COMHAIRLE CHONTAE ÁTHA CLIATH THEAS
SOUTH DUBLIN COUNTY LIBRARIES

COUNTY LIBRARY, TOWN CENTRE, TALLAGHT
TO RENEW ANY ITEM TEL: 462 0073
OR ONLINE AT www.southdublinlibraries.ie

Items should be returned on or before the last date below. Fines, as displayed in the Library, will be charged on overdue items.

2/2/12

Photograph of Mary O'Donnell © Lucan Studios

THE PLACE OF MIRACLES

Mary O'Donnell, originally from Monaghan, lives with her family near Straffan, County Kildare. Her first three poetry collections were published by Salmon Poetry (*Reading the Sunflowers in September; Spiderwoman's Third Avenue Rhapsody; Unlegendary Heroes*). The 2003 collection *September Elegies* was published by Lapwing Press, Belfast. Her fiction includes *Strong Pagans, The Light-Makers, Virgin and the Boy*, and *The Elysium Testament*.

Formerly the *Sunday Tribune*'s Drama Critic, she is a regular contributor to RTÉ Radio and has presented a number of programmes including the European poetry translation series, 'Crossing the Lines'. She is a member of the Irish academy, Aosdána.

MARY O'DONNELL

THE PLACE OF MIRACLES
new and selected poems

**NEW
ISLAND**

The Place of Miracles
First published in Ireland in 2005
by New Island,
2 Brookside,
Dundrum Road,
Dublin 14
www.newisland.ie

ISBN 1 905494 06 8

British Library Cataloguing in Publication Data. A CIP catalogue record for this book is available from the British Library.

Typeset by New Island
Cover design by New Island
Printed in UK by Athenaeum Press Ltd., Gateshead, Tyne & Wear

New Island receives financial assistance from
The Arts Council (An Chomhairle Ealaíon), Dublin, Ireland.

10 9 8 7 6 5 4 3 2 1

For Adrianne Marcus, poet and friend

I would like to thank the editors of newspapers, journals, magazines and anthologies who first published poems from previous collections.

Acknowledgments are made to the editors of the following publications in which certain poems from *The Place of Miracles* first appeared: *Poetry Ireland Review, The ShOp, The Stinging Fly, The Laois Anthology, Agenda, Artlife (Ca), Poetry Salzburg, Pelagos, La Colpa di Scrivere, Sud-Est Kultur (Moldova).* Acknowledgment also to Cliodhna Ni Anluain of *Sunday Miscellany*, where several poems were broadcast.

Contents

Introduction

These poems were written over twenty-three years. They are the result of my preoccupations, my sense of necessary distance from my own biography. There was often no other way to respond but through poetry — at least, no way that offered the same satisfactions and occasional resolutions. I consider myself privileged to find myself today in a country that remains supportive of the foot-soldiers of imagination, finding us occasionally necessary. Are we like fairground mirrors, I wonder? We who find that the making of art is central to our lives? Is our gift to distort the literal reflection, not alone for ourselves but for anyone who cares to look?

In the context of whatever may be refracted from the selection within these pages, I can best qualify that idea by describing it as a light wave, because each book felt very different to me, carrying me on from poem to poem, sweeping me up in its particular energy with all the force of an Atlantic wave.

A poem is the most commonplace thing in the world, giving voice to the commonplace subconscious which might otherwise languish in half-remembered dreams or ill-expressed fragments of emotion. When feeling fails in ordinary speech to do the work of being human, sometimes a poem steps into the void. It is so gentle we scarcely feel its breath, its light, its life. I can think of no other reason to write poems than that the world — brutalised yet still intricate and beautiful — moves me to want to speak back to it in words, that they are my light burden, my alchemist's bag, usually open.

Mary O'Donnell
May 2006

from
Reading the Sunflowers in September,
1990

Antarctica

I do not know what other women know.
I covet their children; wardrobes
stocked with blue or pink, froth-lace
bootees for the animal-child
that bleeds them.

Their calmness settles like the
ebb-tide on island shores –
nursing pearl conch, secret fronds
of wisdom, certitude.
Their bellies taunt.

I do not know what other women know.
Breasts await the animal-child.
I want – maddened by
lunar crumblings, the false prophecy
of tingling breasts, turgid abdomen.

Antarctica: The storm petrel hover;
waters petrified by spittled winds:
Little fish will not swim here.
Folds of bed-sheet take my face.
Blood seeps, again.

"But you are free", they cry,
"You have no child" – bitterness
from women grafted like young willows,
forced before time. In Antartica,
who will share this freedom?

Cot Death

When I turned her over,
what I saw was a changeling's mask,
mauve and mottled, like old lilac,
her lips purpled shut.

No flutter from her eyelashes
that always quivered
like down on a young bird,
and I knew how her nostrils,

the pink-edged membranes,
were inhabited by death,
how the sculpting of her ears
had nothing now to do with sound.

Since then, I am haunted awake,
a wailing behind my temples,
and I grit my teeth each time
I see dolls in snug shop windows,

their glassy eyes accusatory,
knowing them to be corpses
subpoenaed for a public enquiry
into some woman's unmotherly neglect.

I will always wonder if
those matrons who shun me lest
I conjure a changeling to their doors,
are not correct, I will wonder

if I invoked some blood-curdling sprite
to suffocate the child before she

suffocated me. And wondering,
I am haunted, I am unstill,

my days waxing murderously.

Excision

She grapples in child innocence, mad
with hysteric hurt as the women hold
her down and bind with florid pain:
The cropping of pink lips, curling

coral from screaming girls. Rout
of beaded hyacinth, the weave and
cluster; maize-mornings scythed
by a midwife's halting swipe;

sources dammed like well cast
witchery, before dust days have
frisked in the sun's eye – the
sapping thrust of being honestly

alive: The brothers kick dust at
the sun, run like antelope beyond
the tent. Inside, a stitched stump,
a botched hole, pain that cannot

levitate beyond itself, fear of
woman's pleasure, blocked sun-tide of
the matriarchy, seeping fissures on the
dam wall. On it runs, riddles,

cutting the world's women: Razor
in Sudan, yashmak in Tehran,
purdah in India,
two tongues for Japan.*

Here, veiled tranquillity, the
splice and fever of diet and clean

hair, fragrance, spruce linen;
children, gleaming, scrubbed clones,

excised like her, the genie in
little heads mopped of mystery
till they too live a crisp anxiety.
Neither goddess nor woman inhabit

this temple for which earth is carved,
but diamond fortitude, covert moments
trickling to crow's feet, gimlet eyes
which mirror sparkling smiles. It rots

the brightest soul until she
is too cuntless to dare, too numb
to snare the trancing of
voluptuous years that bled her

white and loathe to fight.
Her torpor fractures the wall.
Fissures creep, the sun-tide
rises even as she sleeps.

Razor in Sudan,
yashmak in Tehran,
purdah in India,
two tongues for Japan.*

* In Japan, there is a male and female version of spoken Japanese:
Men may use both conventions, whereas women may use the female
version only.

Reading the Sunflowers in September

These days she walks to the sunflowers.
You never know whether she'll make it,
her bones having grown in recent times.
Such starvation is an art:
Admire her craft as she upbraids
a summer gluttony, tears sheets from herself,
inspired by shrinkage.

She reads sunflowers daily,
the spindles of her fingers reach out,
stroke yellow ellipses
as if each petal were a sign.
What really holds her are the seeds,
tucked tight like critical reviews
within a yellow convention.
They swell and separate while autumn
seems to idle, enchant her hunger
all the more, telling tales, gaze
like a thousand eyes at the sun's path.

She is bent on hers,
knows what she creates will have it all –
the Word made genderless.
These days she walks to the sunflowers.
When the seeds drop,
when petals shrink to skeletal,
she'll have made it.

Women's Rites

After breakfast, we sit and eye
each other, steaming tea-cups
clasped in reverent hands.

With suspicion. Mother and daughter
cast bait across a brown expanse of table,
await the first ripple of secrets.

They nibble cautiously; then spill
in full cascade on sifting ears.
Flash-torrents of intimacies

to cleanse our anchored hearts.
It is quiet; the ticking clock
a metronome of understanding nods

and adroit stares.
A woman's time.
No men to share the rites

as we anoint ourselves
at the Niger. Inky violet.
Warywise we tread, lest lips

unleash some brimming fury
to ferry us on darker streams
of spite. We sing hieroglyphs,

penalise in tongues till
hair is cropped and time sits
glacial on the skin.

Fragile women. Fearful then,
ascend to mooring pools
and sip our tea, at peace.

Brief wickedness absolved,
we reassure with banter.
Teeth strain the last mouthful.

A smile. Our cups are empty.
We wash up, cradling new insights.
Crafty women. We know our rites.

Herald

Because the sun seems to slip
off the edge of the world,
each day plays earnestly on light,
birch-leaves like lanterns,
black hedges festooned with rain.

Starlings and rooks come into their own,
wait on dead branches
as the yellow wheel slows,
aware of a vixen near the coop,
stalking cats that lurk in the field.

I listen to what they say
in the light of short days,
read signs in the sky,
how star-maps yield
to wet vapours at dawn.

I watch for a figure
coming through mist, striding,
striding with great news to tell,
his hands empty,
the sun cresting his wild head.

Histories

1.

You can drift through Europe for weeks,
till your eyes glaze from the ache
of stuccoed ceilings, frescoed façades,
poems and dedications in an arc of colour
above a doorway, bannered from one century
to another, like letters of praise.

Half-dazed by the casual abundance
of cornices, architraves, rose-windows,
you read a story in stone, feel the breath
of incubi from 14th-century gargoyles
that dance in a sunlit cupola, perch
on the symmetries of a Gothic arch.

The perfect clocks in German cathedrals,
all yellow sun and moon, burnished planets,
computed in a space the size of a tablecloth,
a people's soul ticking coherently
in patient mechanics, in slate and stone,
like a message to the future.

2.

Coming home to Ireland is to feel deprived
in the pretty reds of a Georgian square,
the tamed aesthetic of wrought-iron balconies,
to sense this place an afterthought
of recent history, straggled haphazardly
across the ramparts of a few square miles.

It is to drive through a country village,
know every house was once a servant's hovel,

to let your anger leak on sodden thatches,
on scutched acres at the edge of a bog –
written about, loved like a mistress,
but – for all the cant – triflingly.

3.
Ireland reads no glorious hieroglyph beyond
a code of cashels and scarred fields,
mumbling efforts to minister a hunger,
hears no clarions where steep roofs
brush the clouds, or great prisons
are stormed in the name of freedom.

No sense of early birth, or the way
a street is loved for its yellow decay,
the secrets of memory laid down
in generations of tramping feet, or
the bell-flung echoes of those who rushed
to write themselves on history's scroll.

Deprived of a morning chance to admire
in rites of praise, this place
never stretched its limbs while young,
or sang deep-roofed cacophonies,
loosed reasons to deck itself in pride,
whet its tongue unflinchingly in stone.

Savignyplatz, Enniskillen

What I intended was a poem about Savignyplatz,
Berlin, images of black olives saltysmooth
from a Greek restaurant, rough wines,
turgid linden-trees, trains rumbling,
the glances of evening lovers

who have not lain beneath the same white sheets,
instead there is Enniskillen
like the only honest wound in all my poetry,
a collapsed hall, tangled puppet-hole,
instead of wine the smell of singed skin and blood,

those olives were bitter as gall anyway,
Savignyplatz, where we observed a couple
who had not lain beneath the same white sheets,
I knew by her pretence of fright when he
crept up behind, you by his ardent attention,

how he took nothing for granted, but they did
in Enniskillen on Remembrance Sunday,
with poppies in their trim lapels,
and hymns like poems for those
in wars that killed Berliners too.

Now I know how poems explode in the face
if you think they're friendly animals,
civil and domestic – once and for all,
shapes slung within white sheets
are human grenades across Savignyplatz,

the black olives saltysmooth are stones
lodged like rubble in my poetic gullet,

Enniskillen is the dead, wide-open wound
of poppy heads, twisted masonry for all my words.

Uncharted

Once, we dreamed
        of sailing the Amazon,
alligator-green, watery light, snakes,
with David Attenborough – far, far
        from the crannóg lakes
of Monaghan, and we considered the merits
        of marrying
the German Chef d'Equipe.
Now we meet perhaps in summer –
        children, work,
the foibles of husbands, jam-packed
in the bolting phrases of a day or two,
        and we know how erosion
has deepened those rivers we never travelled
        with men we have not loved.
Despite time and distance, corners knocked,
part of us is still girlish, still rafted
        in a state of half-want,
well-primed for awkward water,
just in case… just in case…

Holiday, 1972

She was a wounded woman,
lived in the hills
above the village,
       a writer, alone.
Kind and warm,
skin etched by fine lines,
she gave me three silver rings
after a game of pub poker,
talked
       as if I knew the world,
of films, books and Vietnam,
the desire-filled space of America.

She'd pass our house,
       half-doped, eyes distant,
the gently silting finger of Dunmanus Bay
somehow missing her.
Sometimes
       my mother gave her stew,
then she'd move on,
her loping, liberal walk,
body slim and jeansed,
       with a rabbit on her shoulder.
It was dying, its eyes ran, blind
though she wouldn't believe it.

In the evening, musicians from Cork
played jigs and reels,
their eyes danced knowingly
as they piped and fiddled,
       feral behind the jollity.
She'd walk to the hills above the bay,

carrying the rabbit.
One of them would follow,
entering her kindnesses,
stilling a rawness
in the hours before dawn.

Cycling With Martin

This harvest, we whirr across terrain
    once dreamt of, cautious immigrants
        in the land of forgotten love.

Miles breeze past our heads,
    unfasten a week's tidy thoughts
        as we eye the possibilities

in tumbling thickets,
    or sample blackberries,
        find more than sweetness,

a reckless tang bruising the lips.
    I sample your body on such trips,
        draw urgent images from leaves,

long, pushing mushrooms, flaming rosehip,
    idle on the hours we've spent,
        the heat of your buttocks

as you break within me.
    Windflown now, the bikes
        sheer down the last stretch.

This bawdy autumn, I quicken,
    feel vintage warmth in the sun,
        unsprung from myself as the year drowses.

Hungry for peaches and plums,
    flesh lustily cloven,
        I repeat my cyclist's mantra,

brute labials like *love, my love…*

The Art Room

In early June, all that remains
are puppets and forgotten dolls.
Punch and Judy slouch on a shelf,
doll monks and nuns are sharp-faced demons
in flailing serge; in an open window,
the Three Wise Men wear swathes of red,
all wisdom to the winds
as a butterfly wavers by.

A place of stick figures,
papier-mâché faces,
the bright folly of discovery
in shaky swirls of yellow,
spatters of purple and green.
And in one corner, the portrait of a girl,
the brush-stroke of some tender technician
who yet must learn the flagrant daubs,
exotic trials of colour
on the hot palette of days.

from
Spiderwoman's Third Avenue Rhapsody,
1993

Flying to the Mericas

I've never crossed so much water,
above high cirrus, milk-haze rendering
to hot sea-plains long ago explored
by men with salt-encrusted lips,
their thundering sails, knife-sharp prows,
potent masts. Drifting west,
glaciers south of Greenland,
slivers and crescents like winking eyes,
golden bellies; finally, Long Island, and
I remember a dream of Indians, paradise,
watch the Atlantic now caul white kisses
on the finger of a continent.
Beyond Manhattan, Chicago, Alexandria,
I hear the desperate pounding at roots, weeds,
see brown people protect themselves
with vision-potions, rank, warm oils,
against the gifts and plagues
from the old world's lungs.
Across the land their voices rise:
O Healing Water, Beaver Creek,
Spirit of the Lake, Coon Rapids!

Memo to God over Chesapeake Bay

October 4. 1991, nine a.m.,
sunlight carves the world
to fall forest, water,
distant, steaming cities.
I glide right over paradise
on an average weekday flight –
I, Your enemy –
my turbulent wings spread wide

over the earthy and forbidden;
that long, north-tilting waterway,
feathered with a trail
of fancy weekend yachts,
questing for bounty
south of Baltimore,
(all the Indians are dead, as You know,
and in Your name).

But tell me why – because
I assert the right to free will –
am I the outcast who listens, gazes,
admires – I, Your equal – left
dodging through shopping-malls, subways,
or hovering in demotic sewers
(like a pervert) pretending
to be what I am not?

My body itches beneath this robe,
racked with uncleanliness.
Word has it that my brother
gets a new sword and shield
every Easter, Michael the Archangel,

while I fester between heaven and hell,
tantalised, in ancient bronze tatters
like some celestial wino!

Funny thing though. Today over
Chesapeake Bay, I knew there wasn't much
to choose between us. The pity is,
You can't acknowledge that – up there
playing the Big Fellow, the People's God.
But I flew forth and mingled,
I learnt the human touch,
kissed babies, appraised their mothers

with an angelic glance, then got drunk
with the fathers.
Those guys feel *comfortable* with me!
What say we talk,
over lunch, tomorrow p.m.
at Baltimore airport?
(I'll be at the control tower.)
Regards to the gang,

Lucifer.

The Swimmers

Loon Lake I called it,
though there were no loons,
the water a gouache of shadow,
ripples, bubble-helixes
you said were snakes,
or snapping turtles.

Boy I called you,
though manhood has etched
its fictions on your skin;
all the way back from the raft,
you swam within reach,
knowing the distance scared me.

Topaz light flushed the trees
to first fall passions,
the water smelt of sap and silt,
that long swim an initiation,
my limbs flexing effortlessly
in the deepest stretch before the pier.

Scenes from the Gulf Breeze

The moment I step inside that train
I feel a thrumming in my head,
seduction
in the amber necklet
on the throat of a man opposite.

At five in the morning,
frequencies build;
garlic, jambalaya, chowders;
I catch the tread of New Orleans,
the drums, the shiny-breasted women.

The train shoots past watermelons,
pumpkins, a galaxy of suns,
chinaberry trees,
steaming tracks
fondled by kudzu.

In the dining-car, a party,
dark beer and Southern Comfort.
I drink to all my journeys,
to dust the colour of crushed grapes,
and red-cotton, back-pack days.

All around, that grey, slate skin,
women in fake furs, their earrings
swaying, the scented men
with tilted hats, delicious throats
made for slow kisses.

Spiderwoman's Third Avenue Rhapsody

Allegro appassionato
cantabile e molto tenuta la melodia

Out into swirling September,
across blue night streets,
rumbling Gorgons beneath,
their steam raging through man-holes,
or cracks in kerbs.
The drumming of Manhattan,
      salsa-music,
and me stepping down
at last to inhabit the body
      I forgot I had.

      EXTRA! EXTRA!
Woman Firing On All Four Cylinders!
Third Avenue Bionic Woman!
Woman Released from her own Conundrums!
Suddenly I have lips, limbs, hips,
ears like trumpet-lilies blooming
to the sound of blues and soul,
the throb of bars and restaurants.
Beneath my clothes, new skin,
beneath that skin, oxygen.
The lobes of my lungs breathe city decorums,
antennae sprout from my forehead;
outside, the world staked confidently
      on concrete ladders
      that lead to the stars,
      each rung
a yellow light in someone's window.

Moderato

EXTRA! SPIDERWOMAN SCALES FORTY-
STOREY BLOCK
      legs black-furred and glossy,
she turns, open armed
to view the chimera of a dioxide sunset,
then parachutes down the airways
      on her own web.
EXTRA! EXTRA! SPIDERWOMAN ENTERS
RESTAURANT!
      La Bolina, a hostess
with hoops through her ear-lobes –
the tan – the white smile –
the bright-eyed vacancy that ignores
arachnid appetites,
and yes, yes, yes,
SPIDERWOMAN SELECTS FRESH TUNA
STEAK,
and should I die before I wake
      there is nothing like it,
      nothing, save good sex,
such succulent flakes of flesh,
a salad moist as happy dreams.

Allegro Con Brio
    espressivo

Wined and dined, EXTRA! EXTRA!
SPIDERWOMAN TAKES SUBWAY TO TIMES
SQUARE!
sheds black leggings, her octal scuttle,
      down 42nd Street, the heat,
      the grease, black dawgs
      hunting meat,

'Hey baby, ah suck pussy!' (*cres.*),
his filigree touch at my elbow,
this sandal-footed dandy with cock for sale
and knowing eyes, moves on,
his limbs gyrate too-daah-riddim-babe
(*cres. ff*)
Metropolitan hucksters, sex-menu,

One-Hour Fuck, Family Viewings, Tits-A-Go-Go,
Pussy Galore! Oriental Girls,
Anything U Want!

Chime and cowries tinkle, open doorway,
the rankness of goatskins,
Spiderwoman peers inside (*piu rit.*),
there's the Mandarin of Manhattan,
formerly of Chin-Kuah-Hin, Vietnam,
his extensive whiskers,
his sweet incense,
his child wife,
eyes that know a spider in women's clothing,
his crystals arranged in shimmering codes –
Chinese cures, root-ginger, ginseng,
ground antler, tiger's penis (*dim. e rit.*)
Restores energy, guarantees long life
and potency!

Andante non tanto

Where are you now, Anne Bradstreet,
whadd'ya think of this, proud pilgrim
with your terse verse?
The pussy-suckers, the traders,
this metropolitan chowder, fishy with
Irish, Mexican, Puerto Rican, Asian,

stingless WASPS, Hasidics, Reform, the Jews?
        Look at me, Mistress Anne!
Look! My ears are trumpet-lilies,
my eyes like bowls of sky,
my skin a pond where I have drifted
peacefully, on my back,
a view of the stars
between crags of scrapers!
        Like you, I have come,
I have learnt metamorphosis, I have come,
dewy pilgrim in hope of prodigy,
and look what marvels I have found!
MYSELF! SPIDERWOMAN WALKS ON THE
EAST RIVER!
SPIDERWOMAN DISCOVERS HER SOUL!

Bet you won't approve, Anne babe.
Don't be afraid,
        O ancient Ms America,
        O New England first-corner
with our Bible, and poems
that strained for voicing!
You're still there,
right here, among the salsa,
the Bud Light, the crack 'n' the coke,
sure you are,
but you're still changing, baby,
your great savage heart (the one you
thought you'd tamed) smoulders with love
on this demonic estate (*ritard.*),
        this dreaming, ocean prominence,
        this violet, scandal-lit place,
        this beautiful fakery,
        O wild Manhattan! (*cres. ff*)

The Rib

The man has always shadowed me,
grey to his skin,
his eyes shut as he stands behind me,
imagining he owns me.

What gave them the idea
that I was spawned from a rib?

Why not tell the truth,
that I am daughter
of wide skies, wheatfields
to the horizon,
my buttocks impressed gently
on southern clouds,
my joy in the thrush's throat,
my ecstasies in veins on leaves,
in teeming green-ness
and balls of midges,
furious with lust beneath apple trees.

Life itself spawned me,
not the wedge of bone,
I am singular as he is,
and so alone.

Eve in Eden

Primitive from long wintering,
she takes first steps
and nothing repeated,
dazzled by spurting impressions –
a man she is bound to ignore,
sparrows hurtling through clouds,
a growth-ignited world,
forsythia flares and daffodil tract,
the primitive sun
in every living thing.

Her first spring,
first crops are seeded,
first crows rise through the dawn,
a white spatter of lilac buds,
plum-shoots like pearls,
and this first, bewildering man,
she is bound to love.
Having come to her senses,
naked to all creation,
there is nothing she cannot do.

Eve to Adam

To set my hands, soft
around your head, fingerslick
to the roots of your hair,

test the cheekbones,
trace the songlines
along your temples.

Even the stars are in quest,
night fields crackle with frost,
earth-gods arouse deepest clay.

Primed for seasoning,
Aries blazes fire and sap
through thickets of long hours,

storms what was smooth,
splits primeval fissures.
Days billow towards light.

Turn your face, the silken eyelids,
close to mine, undo
my breast shield,

mother-of-pearl incised
with fish, snakes,
a flickering firebird.

To set my fingers, soft,
across your mouth,
to open you to kisses –

sun-snood, river of light,
moon-gold at midday,
high summer in the night!

Eve, Discovering Frost

I have slept in this place,
having heard the voice of a man,
lay openly, pondered a song
that kept galaxies glinting
from chill carousels.
Feeling safe, I rested.

At dawn, his touch had plaited
my hair, my shoulders bore
skins of filigree.
All around, the tamarind, the carambola,
in bright sheaths, their fruits
crystalled in the sun.

Mists rose from the garden,
a silver orb split to halves of light.
My dreams having spun the world
to flosses, I cried out,
then uttered one quiet word:
Beloved.

On Revelation

The maps were laid out,
spread before me long ago
in dreams
when I ran from giants:
rivers especially, one
in particular,
diverted from society;
this need to pronounce,
like new speech,
a tongue set free,
is stronger, more peaceful.
Seduced by birches,
an empty boat without oars,
laughter,
I will travel,
an original pilgrim
who has seen
something
in cloud-ships,
ripe leaves,
the dripping wind.

Couples

Whether it is months or years,
you are never sure.
Either way it is all
a matter of time,
before the whole intricate fabric
gives, a wasp's nest exploding,

that cindery, wrought webbing
blasted to the winds.
A slow siege begins,
assuaged occasionally
by kind words,
the well-meant caress.

In the end none of it has mattered.
You retreat,
imagine yourself founding a new colony,
autonomous lover turned atheist,

believing nothing, nothing.

Destination Unknown

This warmest night of the year,
the dusty prickle of uncut grain
wafts at our cheeks.
We drive with windows down
and talk about the tropics,
like strangers
accustomed to travelling alone.

The moon races us to the Curragh,
we cross the plains like Niamh and Oisín,
on the backs of horses
with wild grass for manes.

There are silences too,
crepuscular edges to our chat,
purple horizons within our reach.
The Perseids spit and sizzle overhead,
content to be unheard,
colluding,
burning lights smote on the dark,
pitted against time.

The Crows Rewrite the Gospels in Maynooth

By late October, crows write poems
in the clouds, unadulterated texts
for anyone who dares to look.
They draft first notes silently,
in fields, speculative beaks
transcribe leaf-rot, limp grass, soil.
Later, wrapped in gloomy cloaks,
they rest on electricity pylons,
flap their wings, frighten
the soul's dark entities into submission.

A timely surge decides it,
dense knots loosen, then clatter airwards.
Crows remember to dot *i*'s, cross every *t*,
as necessary to finished work;
each wingbeat exhorts, contradicts
in soaring certainty –
I am not the Messiah! The End is not nigh!
Do not repent –
the lines are scattered,
freeform subversions lost to the eye.

The Magic Trees

The magic trees, birch, rowan,
enclose the garden.
The womanly soul of the birch
sheds peelings of silver bark,
waxy fingers of catkin,
her delicate arms raised
to question the harmonies
of sun and sap.

The rowan, all clustered bloom,
displays bright balls in summer,
all sap risen, trunk
and branches smooth and erect,
lineaments set from first planting,
colours drawn from stormy moons,
or the sun of a winter dawn,
whenever we withdraw behind walls:
life's intention, set
to praise, protect, hand on.

Kildare

In summer it's a huge ship
swaying on tides of wind and cloud.
Grain-fields are decks weathering to gold,
the trees are masts with leaves for sails.
They whoosh heavily, then
tip us over the horizon to the east.
We visit the Danube and Nile,
observe the Ganges delta
silting mud and shed skin,
peelings and leavings of those who wave,
curious that we inhabit such space.
Buoyed contentedly on rigged hours,
the whole world shifts before us.

Maynooth College Chapel Altar, Viewed from the Gallery

Someone's idea of gothic heaven,
cut from a dream of Michelangelo,
seven spires, celestial signposting.
Backed by nets of gold,
the lineaments of idolatry
thrust at halcyon ceilings,
choir and musicians levitate
on the Brahms *Requiem.*
The moonstone curves,
tawny nodules on every pinnacle,
are footholds for the minor gods,
called at short notice
by spiralling Hosannas
to view the underworld.

Maynooth College, August

A cloistered place.
The drench of lime-flower
on tennis-courts of a summer evening.
New clerics, peach-fuzz on chin
    like sleep in the eyes of children,
    fervently soutaned.

From the Bible –
doves, pampas-grass, a sundial.
From sleep to sleep a mystic cloying.
The monkish garden, florid blooms,
    streams, capricious ghosts.
    I love and loathe such places:

echoes of purple twilights
on crumbled tennis-court,
the occult haunt of bats and owls.
A hard game, watched, applauded
    by tubercular boys
    from a silent century,
their graves and little crosses
the resting place of swallows.

In Search of the Woman of Allen

1.

Between Clane and Prosperous,
the veil comes down,
neither mist nor rain,
the road a switchback ride
across the first sweep of bog.
My certainties undone:
the end of the world,
hemispheres of earth and sky,
only bleak hostelries,
for Heathcliff and Catherine to dream.

What places, what names!
Prosperous.
And who has prospered?
Have they prospered in love?
In tempests of birth? In dying?
Burger-joints – gotcha baby! –
the undertaker,
the auctioneer,
the supermarket,
homes with baronial names.

2.

Open country after,
no longer a serious part
of the Pale.
Peatland gravity drags me,
close (to hell with what I want),
the road pitted, swaying;
steep ditches, gorse,
wild broom like trumpets in yellow,

forget the shops,
forget unchallenged safety.

The traces intensify –
magic trees, rowans, hazels,
druidic forces –
divine me, black fecundity!
Diabolical winds. The roots
hold fast beneath peaty skin.
Allenwood, *Fiodh Alúine,*
short straggle, shops, a pub,
the cooling tower,
a mud urn from a giant potter's wheel.

3.
I gear down,
unhurried beneath
hunchbacked hedges,
trees blown to scimitar blades
by a caprice of elements.
Hill of Allen, earth-hump high,
Fionn Mac Chumhail, the Fianna;
young Caoilte
might have stretched his legs
in such a ligulate wood.

Behind, the black bog
seeps, patchy between trees,
firebrand-gorse,
an ancient archipelago,
place of spirits,
hosts of the streaming dead,
will o' the wisp lights,
night-motes,

a babble of history
somewhere beneath.

4.
Then Clonbullog, *Cluain Bollóg*,
Meadow of the Loaf of Bread,
my full, delicious
sight of bog,
black bread of plenty
to fill starving bellies.
The sun pours incense,
there are whispers in bushes,
older voices, urgent chatter.
I hear! I hear!

The Bog of Allen,
fringed with wild cotton,
heather, low flowers,
rape crops blown to weed
in golden spatters.
Black, jet-black to the horizon,
I sink with every step,
like walking on carpets in the
Oriental Hotel,
then wade on,

suspecting the earth takes a fancy
to my body –
she might part her lips
and swallow me whole,
I might disappear
into the wet, matted deep.
The yellow machines
trundle the length of it –

bagging peat,
tornados of clouds in their wake.

5.
Some day, some day,
they might yet dig her up,
my ancestor to the power of n,
down there,
among roots long dissolved
to dense, black solids!
I sense skeletons,
the skull of Allen Man,
femur of Allen Woman,
the smooth sockets

of her pre-Christian pelvis,
light-boned receptacle
once filled with glistening bowel,
or a foetus,
bone-fragments like moon-dust,
my ancestor to the power of n!
How she repels me too,
her dread, aged chemistry,
her residues infecting the wind,
warning of intruders.

A chance to peer
at a fossil-image, my own:
a place of oak-wood, elk,
wolves, wild dogs,
people young in history,
the smell of their fires
drifting across midland forests,
the lardy stench of their meat,

its sizzle and drip,
chins glistening by tallow light.

But this woman repels,
I know her – insistent –
myself – perhaps too well
to dig deeper.
Allen Woman stirs, restive
in her sub-terrestrial vein,
bids me depart this sunken lair,
ebony bog-bower,
her arrowy bones
pointing at the sky.

The Journey

I
The Moment

It is not like the old masters.
No wavering halo,

like jellyfish
in a sea of grace;

no wingbeat brushing close,
or tremor of lilies

from some heart-lurching emissary.
Instead, the May sun

shoots bronze rivets at buttercups,
the sunchair will not support

this unburdening slumber.
Stretched flat

beneath the ash,
she hears a distant circus

cross the fields from the east,
with drums and trumpets,

then loud, raucous cymbals,
and carolling voices,

and tambourines closer,
and bells on painted elephants,

as they break the young corn
in a noisy caravan,

the riot and ring-dance
of naked acrobats

cartwheeling close
to her indolent flesh.

II
The History of Seasons

Time is retarded,
winter immobilises.
Details are imprecise,
I drift in an undead slumber.

Even if I forget,
already the child is remembering.
Its head inverts thought,
absorbs memories from bones,
sockets, the softening ligaments.

Each time I pause,
mulling fragments
lost to the previous day,
a kick rakes the tight glaze
of my abdomen;

I come to my senses
at the prod of an elbow.
Occasionally, the bones of her fingers
score question-marks –

little hooks, they will
flush me out
in the high summer of a January night.
After, it will be my turn to remember.

III
Third Trimester Interlude

It feels like nothing in particular,
certainly not like any fruit,
no plum or pink-fleshed pear,
is neither beautiful nor ugly.
Perhaps the spark behind my eyes
is less than mercurial
(one does not gleam
with such definite humours),
but that is all.
Still, I think of Michael Douglas,
often, often,
dream of full, swaying branches,
golden canopies of fruit,
I linger more than usual over the
planes of your back and thighs,
want to be petted, stroked, held,
kissed, licked, sucked and juiced,
till I am shining silver.
I can hardly see below my belly,
but it is not troublesome, no,
not in the least,
nor thoughts of you
and Michael Douglas,
the three of us happy on the bough
of the tree of life.

IV
The Shadow World

Unaccustomed to shade,
wary of greys, gouaches,
half-lit spectres,
I admit the world has changed.

This body, they say,
is for the living.

At least dreams are lush
with everything I miss.
By day, dullness drifts invisibly,
a pollen-borne disease,
I scarcely feel the wind on my face,
wines are like meths; garlic,
tandooris and pungent cheese
are nightmarish plots
from a world I once knew.
Did I really live there?
Did I eat that tack?

When can I go back?

Pre-Birth Flirtation with Self and Others

The night before,
I worked my hair till it bushed
thick and shining,
I made-up with care, donned
a damask nightgown
for my final sleep.

Perched on the hospital bed,
I waited in a turquoise robe
with red and golden birds of paradise;
wafting perfume,
I cracked jokes
with the chap who emptied the bins.

'Gorgeous' he called me,
which is how I felt.
I knew I'd need every armour,
every shield, skill and artifice
for the coming day,
mostly to remember who I was,

what I could be,
in the time of good blood.
Flailed into battle,
self versus self,
versus death,
versus love and fear,

the complacent deceit
(or was it kindness?)
of woman after birth
flared up.

In those moments
when I thought
I would burst, hands and nails

ridged blood-sweet,
I pushed
to the edge of oblivion,
pushed to the edge of my life,
pushed for her,
only for her.

Daughter

For years I have called
across great distances,
feeling her hover
beyond demotic streets,
the summer dust,
the slanting rains.

I have called to her
across miles of fields,
thinking I glimpsed her
in drenched grasses,
or near a poppy
in shimmering oats.

Now she sets out
from some wild galaxy:
as I sleep, she nears,
testing glints of starlight,
nights of hollow soul.
I have called her to be human.

Now she comes.

Survival Tactics

Sucking furiously, her eyes
bore through me, unwavering.
The kid's been here before,
more experience in her eight weeks
than I've managed in half a life,
knows how to look you straight
in the eye without smiling,
hedging her bets
until hunger pangs retreat,
the bottle half-empty.
Then, the smile that melts icebergs,
raises sea-levels, could
sink the Netherlands,
or drown half of London.
Cooing kindness,
she ghost-wrote *How to Win Friends
and Influence People*,
learnt in a previous existence
that bees are caught
with honey, not vinegar.
And so are mothers.

Shipwrecks and Stories
(for Anna, b. 20 January 1993)

In the nights before birth
when the moon was full,
word came of a stricken tanker
in the Shtelands, TV pictures
of slack-feathered
oil-furred creatures.

On the day of your coming,
a president was sworn in,
messages unfurled, hopes
of freedom, tolerance,
the rights of living and dying.
I thought I would die that day.

The minute hand on the labour ward clock
seized up with my pain.
I tried to sing,
told stories to the midwives.
They'd heard it all before –
the lives of women in birth

never before so compressed
as in that moment,
the clench of truth or lie.
I told stories, spoke slowly
between the pains, spinning fables
to save me, remind me

of who I was. And they did.
At the close of every story,
I repeated one saving phrase,

was delivered from battle:
'I can and I will, I can and I will!'
Believing that, you were born.

In the Shetlands, a tanker
had split in two,
birds and otters slipped into death
as darkness fell.
In Dublin the wet dark threw up our child,
sleek with life.

from
Unlegendary Heroes,
1998

In the Tuileries

We misjudged the scale of things.
Two fifteen or thereabouts, we'd said.
Once off the *rue de Rivoli*, I knew
that we would wander without meeting.
I sat awhile, back to the sun,
watched children send wooden sailboats
jagging at the ornamental pond,
hoped that you'd be drawn to those
who idled near the brittle floats.
An icy autumn day, lethal winds
in a high, blue sky drove fruits
and leaves to withdraw and sink deep.
No reference to a world rank
with injustice, no sense of all the wrongs
and all that stank about the universe.
Here, a place we'd read about,
a novelistic arena, a moment in a season,
where eternally dogs and women breeze
by as if on wheels, and silent couples stroll
the yellowed grit between the trees,
and white-shod tourists like ourselves,
revisit all the chapters that they must.
We balanced as never before, but separately.
In all that vastness between us,
no exclaiming on symmetry or stone,
on sculpture or period; comfort for sure,
in a city endowed, but alone
with orangeries, trim trees in view,
the grand line of paths extended perspectives
beyond the usual limits. You felt it too,
I discovered later, and absence, as if
we'd inadvertently cleared the wrong fence,

then herded one another prematurely, set to fail,
towards some final mortal innocence.
As so often, we misjudged the scale.

One Sunday at Seapoint

for Redmond O'Hanlon

How transparent those crabs
In deathly buckets.
Children dare one another
Down the tide-tossed steps,
A child introduces herself

Over and over, then shrieks
At a maverick wave.
A light wind paws the rim of my hat.
In the bay,
Sails tug like hooks

Against Venetian blue.
Today, a different wildness in me,
Unleashed between snacks
Of ice-cream, crisps.
The children scream,

Possessed by comic djinns
Who hear a tornado,
Sense the centrifugal pull
As bones are driven against my skin.
The child who introduces herself

Over and over,
Runs past my moments of despair,
Arms flailing,
Voice rising in hilarity.
I lean forward on shingle

That grinds into panicking palms,
Bare heels.

Remember this, I whisper,
The teeth-like yachts,
Nibbling breeze,

Deft run of a retreating tide,
That original smell –
Kelp or brine –
When all the rest is forgotten,
Remember the child,

Crabs, minnows,
Children,
The transparency
Of imprint on any moment,
Those spectral watermarks.

French Fields

The first time I saw sunflowers
In a field, I knew the difference.

Our forced Irish ones,
Rain-shredded, spat on,
Limped in damp yellow
Towards an earwig-flecked harvest.

These French beauties had it all.
We pulled up on the road to Pau,
Stood in a field of yellow heads
That touched and tilted.

Magenta clay, tensile stems,
Those specked brown eyes –
A single dark depth of pupil
For every flower-head

Made love to by the sun.
They turned and turned
In a slow dance of yellow veils,
Acres and acres of simmering girls,

All eyes on the one man
They wanted to ravish
In mid-day fires,
A throb of cricket's wings.

Mme Hoffman's Lemon Tree

The leaves shone,
Clustered around each poised lantern
As we sipped aperitifs
In a windless garden.

When Mme Hoffman wasn't looking,
I let one lemon brush my hand,
Sensed the trembling, clear juices
Hugged within, an enviable tang.

My teeth went wet with the need
To bite, my eyes closed
At the prospect
Of colour, oil, acid.

I withdrew slowly,
Heard the sudden intake.
A whispered *Non, Madame!*
Pardon, I murmured,

as if the tree had spoken.

My Father Waving

In the New Year, we drove away from
the house on the hill.
It was shrinking, shrinking,
encased in ice, fragments of Christmas
in winking fairy-lights.
My father waved with both arms
like Don Quixote's windmill.

From the brink of motherhood,
lives swept past,
scuttled on reefs of the present;
then a processional: quiet generations
moved through evening ice the colour of Asia,
parents of parents like Russian dolls
re-entered my body, telling
what was never told anyone,
announcing it now to my unborn girl.

The unstill past entered, forgotten
ghostlings and wanderers fussed
and made ready for the future –
one step ahead, bridging dawns and
afternoons between birthdays and Christmas.
The vision displaced the crammed wells
of my fear. The child turned beneath
my ribs, the parents of parents waved.

The Woman of the Lough

People would talk about getting out
Of situations, or facing up to things,
About cute hoors or brave wee souls.
She always said perhaps, maybe,
We'll see how it works out.

But late one summer night, she went.
Few saw her wade in, or recognised
The yellow swimsuit, the red rubber hat
With half-perished daisies.
The water was like silk on her chest and arms,

That border lake smelt sweet
With secrets as she front-crawled
To the deeps they said were bottomless.
All those dawn swims amounted
To something, the frustrated pleasure

Of being on her own, an hour between
The panic of a teething baby
And the habit of a husband's face.
At least she got the swimming right.
Dipped duck-arsed, learnt to hold rage

As long as it took.
Deeper she went, further and deeper,
Across the silent lough,
Smiled to herself when she glimpsed
The bottom they said wasn't there.

Greenish brown, matted sludge,
Then patches of sand, the fish avoiding

Her. She was afraid of nothing.
The night she left, she dove beneath,
Emerged at the far side, newborn,

Slid into the waiting car.
By the time the boats came,
She was long gone.
Her swimsuit, her hat,
Floated in the dark.

Years later, she returned from Scotland.
People said she'd risen from the grave.
'And will y'stay?' her husband wondered.
'Perhaps. Maybe.
We'll see how it works out.'

Unlegendary Heroes

'Life passes through places.'
– P.J. Duffy, *Landscapes of South Ulster*

Patrick Farrell, of Lackagh, who was able to mow
one acre and one rood Irish in a day.
Tom Gallagher, Cornamucklagh, could walk 50
Irish miles in one day.
Patrick Mulligan, Cremartin, was a great oarsman.
Tommy Atkinson, Lismagunshin, was very good at
highjumping – he could jump six feet high.
John Duffy, Corley, was able to dig half an Irish acre
in one day.
Edward Monaghan, Annagh, who could stand on his
head on a pint tumbler or on the rigging of a house.

— 1938 folklore survey to record the local people
who occupied the South Ulster parish landscape.

*

Kathleen McKenna, Annagola,
who was able to wash a week's sheets, shirts
and swaddling, bake bread and clean the house
all of a Monday.

Birdy McMahon, of Faulkland,
walked to Monaghan for a sack of flour two days before
her eighth child was born.

Cepta Duffy, Glennan,
very good at sewing – embroidered a set of vestments
in five days.

Mary McCabe, of Derrynashallog,
who cared for her husband's mother in dotage,
    fed ten children,
the youngest still at the breast during hay-making.

Mary Conlon, Tullyree,
    who wrote poems at night.

Assumpta Meehan, Tonygarvey,
saw many visions and was committed to the asylum.

Martha McGinn, of Emy,
who swam Cornamunden Lough in one hour and a quarter.

Marita McHugh, Foxhole,
whose sponge cakes won First Prize at Cloncaw Show.

Miss Harper, Corley,
female problems rarely ceased, pleasant in ill-health.

Patricia Curley, Corlatt,
whose joints ached and swelled though she was young,
    who bore three children.

Dora Heuston, Strananny,
    died in childbirth, aged 14 years,
    last words, 'Mammy, O Mammy!'

Rosie McCrudden, Aghabog,
noted for clean boots, winter or summer,
    often beaten by her father.

Maggie Traynor, Donagh,
got no breakfasts, fed by the nuns, batch loaf with jam,
the best speller in the school.

Phyllis McCrudden, Knockaphubble,
who buried two husbands, reared five children
and farmed her own land.

Ann Moffet, of Enagh,
who taught people to read and did not charge.

The Girl of 1960

When the crunch came,
her natural mother didn't want to meet.
A middle-aged woman
not much older than her daughter
would not greet her firstborn,
dared not unpick the well-darned tear
    in a life uprooted in disgrace.

Now gentle, raging Margaret
sails the world in quest of mothers
who'll say *yes, you are good, you are
the best child ever, how I love you!*
She wants mothers –
great peacock's tails of them,
    believing blood is thicker than water.

But one look
the other side of wise sayings,
plasma's as thin as H_2O,
and heart-bonds await her willing
entrapment. Perhaps in the end,
she must mother herself.
    To her it comes sooner than to others.

Eventually, lost mothers
are found as found ones
are slipped loose
from the skin of generations.
Know that, raging Margaret,
lost gentle girl of 1960, know
    all the mothers who think you are *good.*

45 Dublin Street

for my mother, Maureen

In the dream, I am back
in my grandmother's kitchen,
The range oozes
waves of porridgy heat,
stewed tea.
Newspapers are fanned
in an arm-deep window sill.
Outside, a clotted path
of saxifrage runs riot.
The walls are as then,
neutral emulsion
in an evening gloom.

Unlike then,
all is silent.
There are dream-props:
sofa, the long table,
a cut-glass sugar bowl,
that step into the sinister well
of a dark hall.

The symmetry of what is not,
what has been.
I remember.
Some nights I return
and sit, puzzled

by the silence,
and a grey spiral,
like flies, where human traces
still fizzle on the air.
Only the saxifrage grows.

Materfamilias

My grandmother had thirteen pregnancies,
Nine full-term. She, who came orphaned
At nineteen from Clogher to Monaghan,
Fell to undreamt streams of constant parenting:
Keeper of children's needs, keeper of spouse,
Two uncles, a doting, whispering grandmother.

In that tall-storied town house, place of
Darkened stairwell, high, mysterious attic gloom,
Beds with bolsters, a sunny, summer sitting-room,
She learned to rule an embattled roost,
Bartered away diphtheria, TB from her brood
Between two world wars and after.

A pansy-eyed flapper, she tended to herself
Obliquely, in astrakhan, or snug suede shoes;
Ambitious for all, yet slow to praise for fear
Of spoiling with Hollywood notions, child-dreams,
Songs she herself was not allowed. Wintering ended
When grandchildren came along, and she grew mild.

By then, with two sons dead, she wore Queen Mother
Hats, like turquoise shells askance
On venerable hair. Would she do it all again,
My mother once asked. No chance, she said,
Womanhood, the struggle between self and others,
Was costly; to deal once with the rise and fall

Of life, of death, enough.

This Child, This One

A stake through the heart
impaling us to the counsel of flesh,
a command never again to be separate.

       It is like winter,
which imagines withdrawal
from red, whirling days,
almost convinced of slumbering death.

All the time, stirrings.
Even in January, daffodil bulbs
split the earth's skin;
she is mottled and sensitive,
her slumber, a terrible dream
of what is seeding
and pervasive,
of pollens to come,
forbids flirtations
            with word or deed.

Our tongues set free
in an eternal spring,
         we test stems of consonants
between our teeth,

balloons of vowels
            tender in our mouths,
discern the salts, sugars,
that viscous glide
along the tongue's rim.

So we live:
at the edge of spirit,
staked forever to the grace of flesh.

An Island, One Winter

Snow 1

Like love,
born in an instant,
you think you know it
when branches shimmy into light.
It spreads to the soul,
you are taken, ravished
by an idea of intimacy.
Poised for more, then more,
it melts from your glance,
to nothing.
Look out.
The little firs, miserable
at shrinkage,
the loss of nerve.
Snow, love. Never enough.
The fleet earth, cowardly.

Snow 2

The silence of it.
When all the cries are muffled.
Infants. Women. A man alone in his mind,
his car inching down a blue glass motorway.
Lovers. Quenched footfall.
The silence
of a thousand years ago,
cattle shifting, cudding,
in the covered byre.

In snow, we learn distance:
the silence of neanderthals
shuddering in sleep,
survival through tallow,
rindered remains,
an ox tail charred in the flickering night.

After snow,
the hope of whiteness.
A threat of innocence secures us,
the future fizzles
outside the bedroom,
the house: the white roof,
the wings of dreams.

This silence is the future:
an invitation to those minutes
before survivors stir,
before the cries,
again, and again,
as fatal pollens
howl silently through skin.

Our assured legacy
after the trouble of living.

After infants, women,
after the lone men pacing
the dark of their lives.
After the lovers for whom
something was once unblemished,
hope like a branch in snow.

Snow 3

Almost the shortest day.
Sleet whistles to snow. The plum-tree
has claws, and the sundial smothers.
I once finished a novel on a day like this:
that evening in the city, people
deserted cars and walked. Written out
to the last full stop, I was happy to be swaddled
in the night's white chrysalis.

'Whassa?' you mutter now, peering
at the sky. 'That's snow' I say,
then write and re-write. Your hands pound
the damp panes, you are excited
by swags of bushes, the spiralling grey,
soft snow-stars fallen to earth.
Bored now, you crawl to the piano
and suck the pedals.

Soon you're at my knee, tapping,
patting, murmuring. One arm raised,
one finger points. Your eyes beckon.
When I point back, our fingers touch.
But we cannot beam pulses
drawn from sun on this short day,
we are not intimate enough
to tile the planet southwards.

Minute by minute, we meet as strangers,
and I, the absent one, must explain.

Infant
for Martin and Anna

You perch in his arms
and gaze upon us from above,
an Infanta surveying minions.
Something about his strength
is different from mine;
you know it,
feel the full majesty of a good man's arms
sweep you serenely above trifles
like toys and rattles.
Up there, you discover perspective,
recreate for yourself the eyes of callers,
candid, unperturbed. You do not
smile until something is proven.
May the right man always kiss
and hold you.

Promise

I try not to cast too much shade.
Sin would be
to use the excuse
of her growth in my womb,
to imagine her as a limb of myself.
She is her own tree,
late-winter's indomitable shoot.
She takes cupfuls of sun.

I stand well clear
as the branches stretch,
like flutes playing allegros.
Not for anything
would I poison her
with an act of possession,
conceal her from the woodsman
whose task is to make room for all.

Talking to Mum Before Meeting Marie Stopes

That night I phoned, late.
    I wanted to utter it aloud,
        something in my throat

about to slither towards your life,
    like the unformed thing it was,
        red, waxy yellow, a mistake

from the doll factor.
    I stopped of course.
        Your girl grown competent woman

slouched flat on her pillows,
    telephone tucked beneath her jaw,
        all easy mirth and a chuckle on her tongue.

I wanted to tell you
    of this journey, the next day,
        I wanted to pass my heart for safekeeping,

in case this moment
    made of me a doll among dolls.
        I wanted you to remind me

of a rough sweetness,
    the optimism of elder-flowers
        on a summer dawn,

some green excitement
    in my years of running into life.
        I have never been so grown-up, Mum.

I could not tell, even you.
    When we hung up, I checked my holdall.
        I dared not remember the infants.

Would have screamed, my mind
    fixed on thundering glaciers
        in those final hours.

On the wall, the indolent gaze of my Madonna,
    that cerulean cloak,
        the eyes of her remote child.

In another city, you slept.
    Jets came and went, ripping the night,
        stacked hours raided my blood.

I invested in darkness –
    for my life, for asylum –
        and preyed on your presence

that night in the world.

Kate O'Brien Weekender Meets La Leche Leaguers

It was one of me to two of them,
all three of us livid and speechless
after catching the wrong train
at Limerick Junction,
finding ourselves back in that city
of eloquent streets.
We had to talk.
Their eyes were fervent,
their parkas like bronze shields
as they evangelised.
They showed me books, statistics,
proofs – the damning, unforgivable
evidence that society's greatest joy
was to part a mother from her baby.

Then I got going,
my brain ablaze
after delivering a lecture
on The Writer as Storyteller,
oh I was ready, spread my texts,
proofs, the damning, unforgivable
evidence that society's greatest joy
was to part a writer from her words.
'Look at Kate O'Brien!', I thundered,
'Banned! Banned! Banned!'
We sat up all night in the Gleneagle Hotel,
gorged chicken sandwiches and tea;
after, the whiskey,
then the phonecalls.

Anybody. Anywhere. A disgruntled couple
in the 044 area snarled at the La Lechers,
their bed-sheets rustling down the line;
some bloke in 065 breathed heavily
as I told him about my books,
groaned and then hung up.
The next morning we embarked on the correct train,
at the correct time, then parted,
our minds lucid, bearing
gifts we were unsure of,
from beyond the frontiers,
the bones of our lives suddenly exposed.
You could say a useful exchange
had taken place.

Blue Velvet

to a fountain-pen

How the hand seeks balance
Between primitive thumb,
Rhetorical forefinger.
A gracious implement,
Blue and gold,
Her broad, tongued nib
Inscribed.
To write,
To stake a hinterland
On a black-tipped oracle.
Each word reflecting light,
Plays with letters, like a mirror
On a telescope, seizes past years.

The resting eye
Enchanted by filaments of black light,
Coils of syntax like unfolding nebulae.
Through it all she balances,
A sheath of blue velvet,
Contained, rippling
Within maidenly gold hands.

10 Haikus On Love and Death

1.
The man in winter.
His body is a warm cave.
Feel the low fires burn.

2.
Fingers in the soil.
The silent knowledge of roots.
From darkness to light.

3.
They speak of rising.
From what can we rise but death?
Now for the living.

4.
Dog of the spring night,
A frieze of leaves in moonlight,
Frost glitters on fields.

5.
My love's bright flower.
His leaves in a sheen of dew.
His passionate root!

6.
The girls swim like fish.
Hither in the deft ocean.
Minnows seeking warmth.

7.
And if I die now,
Will what is done be enough?
Winter is my judge.

8.
Foxgloves at twilight,
Dipping with purple secrets,
Mauve sheaths drip pollen.

9.
Woman in August.
Her body is a forest.
Here there is welcome.

10.
The red lips of June,
Shirts of sun, ribbons of moon,
How radiant is love!

Bees and Saint Colman

There was one who loved,
watched and handled us

when others feared the hives.
One night as he slept,

a chalice was stolen.
The saint wept for the loss

of the cup of Christ's passion.
We pitied him,

flew to dance a map,
the better that each should tap

the ripest clover,
spotted foxgloves, heather beds

until our sacs were swollen
with a high summer's fill.

Prayer withered his anger;
he almost forgot the sin of theft.

A morning came when,
entering the oratory,

he beheld a newmade waxen form,
a gold, combed, burnished stem,

wrought from our diligence.
He fell to his knees as if bereft.

Again we pitied him,
for his God, his silence,

those indolent prayers that forgot
the passion of our pollen.

Emilia Decorates Waterstown After The Death of Her Son*

There are places for comfort in death.
This is mine.
Go, lackeys, skivvies,
muck-skirted girls
from the hovels of Maynooth,
go home to your broths and breads.

Leave me this – Waterstown –
a cottage for his jest, his play.
These shells I here lay
are the boats of his dreams,
that pearled trail,
oyster like magicked wings,

fantail-festoons of eggs in windows,
quartz and coral
from deeps of earth and sea
entice him to peep here and play
beneath the moonlit cupola.
Marbles and baubles await him.

If I sit in one corner,
behind the threads of a fine marriage,
he will not mind.
If I sit to one side,
playing cards, he'll remember
the half of me, quietly wild,

awaiting some return
in the annex
of my husband's estate;

the other, card-playing half,
loaded and loud
with grief's dice.

* *Emilia Mary, daughter of the Duke and Duchess of Richmond, married James Duke of Leinster in 1747 and went to live at Carton in Kildare. She supervised the alteration of an old thatched cottage called Waterstown into a shell cottage. It is thought that one wall may have been ornamented by Emilia herself, after the death of her son.*

from
September Elegies,
2003

September Elegies

Goodbye!
after Eithne Strong

At this point you are never quite alone.
In twenty years you have never been alone,
have learned to join in, master the civilities,

could be gauged by category,
class, literary output, spouse,
despite the wish for immeasurables,

with the other middle-aged who, committed,
work hard, raise school funds, plan holidays
in difficult locations, meddle in the lives

of their parents. You could iron clothes
at Clapham Junction and not seize up,
the act of negotiation is no problem as you

sort passports, sign forms knowing what you're doing,
politely listen when bored, complain fluently,
looking forward to bed, the sleep of solitude.

You still give a damn, unfortunately.
You look forward to the time when you will not
give a damn. Perhaps at sixty-two

You'll be freed to cast your eye
along the vistas you imagine were denied
by duty, duty, although brief night skies,

fugitive stars, owl-cries in the distance,
lifted your heart as much as pain. A few beloveds,
well-worn, a radiant child, the belief that love
itself is all. These you have held close,
quietly, of course,
never quite alone enough to do it properly.

But love rides on the brink of nothing.
Hope, when none of it will matter – that glance,
that afternoon by a lake of humming dragonflies –

is a route to the best peace of all,
the undressed, the fleshless, the unplagued,
beyond what we imagine as immeasurable –

solitude   silence

Homes
for M.N.

In half sleep, I almost forget that I am here,
and not with you in our own house.
When I open my eyes, a breeze
flickers at the curtains, light pierces,
a lance gleams across the bed.
I take my bearings,
cross the room to look down.

The garden is lit, a spectral daylight,
or an August eclipse
where we compose our lit and unlit sides.
Here, where I grew,
I imagine the ones
who will love and be anguished
together, as families are. Someone

will look down on this garden as I am doing,
in the middle of the night, someone
will be possessed with pleasure and sorrow
at an unannounced hour,
some middle-aged girl or boy
will know everything is borrowed:

a home, a wife's or husband's body – a gift,
as yours has been, your skin ardent as the moon
burrowing across the sky to this room,
far from where you sleep.

Triathlon, Cooley Peninsula

No sheep or cattle above the shore,
but the grazing ghost of a dun bull*
from a story long ago.
Below, at the grey lough, the fit and young
prepare to swim, cycle and run.
A famous athlete signs autographs,
people hover, massaging limbs, stretching quads.
Out for the day, the old couple perch
on the quayside, like two lost land-birds,
scarfed, wool-wrapped, though it is warm.
Suddenly, the swimmers are ready, poised,
they tear in, wading, breasting, free-styling out
and around the pier. Limbs rise and dip,
brown backs arch like speed-crazed carp,
a leader emerges, crawls up the slipway,
uprights himself, sprints towards a bicycle,
pulls on shorts, shoes, is off again.
Through it all, the couple observe,
link one another as if braced
against wind, although the air is still,
the mountain rising, blue above the roofs
of the town. They gaze at the dripping swimmers,
the vigorous sprint towards gleaming bikes.
The woman knots the scarf beneath her chin,
pulls a jacket closely around her shoulders
as if the peninsula were deserted, and they stood
alone. They move slowly, ghosting
among the sleekness of bodies, beside wetness,
salt and stamina. Their feet pick along the cobbles,
cautious around whirring bicycles.
There is nothing to bargain for, nothing
outside the thread of their lives, no bull,
no field, no cause, no possession.

Beyond envy, they pause once,
wonder aloud about these jostling children
whose adult bodies remind them that they too
were once urgent about preening.

Inexplicable that they
once lived so. The story of their lives,
that second, invisible skin, reads like
the myth of Maeve before the facts of history
chased it to the edge – the matter of who owned what,
and who was strongest, such trifling with the spirit,
diversions from what they needed to know:
how to live, and why.

* *The 'dun bull' is a reference to the Táin Bó Cuailnge (Cattle
Raid of Cooley), one of the oldest stories in European vernacular
literature.*

Dawn Rain

Two days ago, in a city hospital,
my father – considering a surgeon's options –
concealed his face in my mother's arms.

Yesterday, a stream of nieces visited,
faces summer-tanned. He wished openly
for more time, spoke of going for broke,

laughed and remembered a July holiday,
the huge drugged pulse of a southern river,
the throb of the cicadas at evening.

This dawn, the rain hisses and gullies
as I too wish for time,
it spills over the house,

a sheath of Egyptian cotton that
encloses us finely as night thins.
The rain drenches house, hospital,

a winding garment of hand-spun cotton
to enfold old kings who wait by rivers,
a faint Babylonian yellow blooms into

my father's skin, tinges trees,
distressing steadily until our feet tread
the downward spin of the wheel of life,

and rain, that September rain,
pushes us further and further
from the sun.

Doctors, Daughters

My mother's small face is wreathed
and criss-crossed by fear. She has
no time for food or sleep.

Away from the hospital,
she rails at us her daughters,
who can do nothing,

her days layered with quests for solutions.
This man, whose pyjamas she irons
and re-buttons, which she brings to him

laundered and crisp, to whom she carries
perfect nectarines, cranberry juice,
is failing her. She wards off visitors

lest they witness his decline,
frantic to capture an antidote,
that special inscribed phial,

to bear it back in her hands
from monstrous caves like a magical gift,
past nurses, past mulling consultants

and, having fought, to shout in scorn:
'See? Fools!' Her every word,
attests to the uselessness of doctors

and daughters, who cannot heal.

The Haircut

'Can you raise your head?' I ask.
He sits, towelled in green beside the radio
as I raise the comb and scissors into the air.

The hair that used to crinkle in curling scripts
around his crown, unheeding of sweet cedar,
grooming oils, is soft as spider's web, like down,

impossible to feel. 'Mind the sideburns,'
he instructs. What I lift in the comb slips and slides,
the scissors barely grasp the ends, indifferent

to the rites of neatness. This hair wants to let be,
extrusions of frail growth lie close to his pores,
stopgaps against escaping ethers.

But I nick and trim, attempting body, bounce
and sheen, while on the radio Albinoni's cellos,
those grave bows, play for us, the forsaken.

Clippings collect along his shoulders, weightless drifts
criss-crossed with metallic strands, like Chinese script
dismantled from the page. Against my will, this fluent

reading of the inevitable, symbols combed from feeble
months. I gather the cuttings, ask my unfleeced father
to hold still, adjust my face before he turns.

Holy

Every venerable ancient seeks out his body,
every ancestor who once struggled
and, themselves inhabited, dwells there.
He almost weeps each time we leave,
then laughs through fear of this encounter
that nothing, no-one, can lift.

His frailty, a habitation for the wise and good,
is suffered in by a suffering god
who waited for a time, a moment,
patient while this son lived in the vastness
of life's green garment, exploring its folds.
Now he draws it down, tightly, closer,
so that the spirit, that vast, tumbling
greenness, the momentous motion of every cell
of his eighty years, are no longer divided,
but live intimately and as one.

Pietà

Nurses drift in, out, faces set to ease
the unrelievable. Already,
his body is settling down to depart: cells
collapse, fluids slow, muscles waste,
the stomach bears no burden,
as if making light for transportation.

'Write about the thirst,' he says,
'for it is awful.' A well-chilled beer,
a walking holiday in Austria –
among his last, hopeless longings,
before the time for talk is over,
and morphine stills the tongue.

Days become the seamless garment
of his breathing which we wear.
The relentless rattle fills the room, our lungs,
as we breathe in time, suction air
to prevent drowning, then the rugged release.

Every exhalation, goes beyond the room,
fills corridors, this hospital, rising cyclical
into the broken clouds outside.
In those long hours, we accompany him,
carrying parcels, wrapped gifts,

his dreams, thousands, one for every
hour of his living.
Death's labour, full-blown,
the clench and squeeze, bears down,
clarifying, haunting. But the heart refuses.

It hammers on, a season
refusing to end, a tree ignoring long shadows,
desperate to bloom. Only breath remains,
essential to this second, pursuing me when I leave
for half an hour, filling my ears
with its urgent phlegm.

That sound undoes the threads of rest,
like an animal dragging through veins, blood,
the minutest filaments, struggling
with him. I cannot sleep. At dawn,
I stir to light from the east, crying gulls,
blackbirds in the shrubbery outside.

Later, everything slows. This day,
he will be born to death. His work
finished, each cell leaf-light. Only the shape
of his skull gives itself still to our hands
as we lean down, down to touch,
to kiss.

This, Pietà, the death-slumped head
falling to a slant of shoulders, nest
of breastbone. 'He's gone,' someone says,
and we look around, bewildered.

Hauntings

A Husband Sleeps

He reminds her of the tombs
of crusaders, full-scale stone effigies,
final rest for men who rode south

to fight the heathen.
The brows are dark and straight,
droop gently towards his temples, meet

the flickering incline of pale eyelids.
The nose is firm, mouth a closed line,
sealed against perfidy of thought or act,

the mind at rest while, around him, infidels prosper.
In dreams, he believes in miracles,
that good will vanquish the unquiet hour,

that serpents shrivel even as they enter
the houses of noble men, while unicorns
graze in his garden, lay pearly horns

in the lap of his lady; she sees him
there, in the weak dawn light,
before the first cars hum to life,

knows the honour of his sleeping time,
how she will never lie beside him on the tomb,
graven lady of silent mouth and rigid limb.

The Sixties Wives
a photograph

In my mother's wallet,
it brings them all to life, those wives
at afternoon tea in the YMCA hall.
Mother and her sister smile out,
cosseted and married, stylish
Chanel navies and a dash of red,
hats with upturned brims.

How lovely the hats! How treacherous
the poise, each woman on the edge of her chair,
around a small table of pink cups and iced buns,
with lumps of sugar that meant an occasion.
The friends beside them smile too,
sparkle at the camera's attention,
Have settled their folded hands,
turned the energy of pale arms
into the dark warmth of their palms.

Later, the prettiest one was called crazy
because she shaved her head,
unable to have what she craved, curls,
elusive power. Later still, her husband's
admiration of another woman's coat
became a monument to her rage.
The rest stayed tranquil as Valium. But she,
extreme to the end, took one step further
and drank weed-killer.

A Marriage
viewed from Dún Aengus

We cross from Ros a Mhíl to Inishmore,
cast spells of salt, rain and sweat,
the shape of an island,
just out of reach.
The trawler, loaded with trippers,
noses currents. Photographs are taken.

Ashore, we persist, impress ourselves
at first on things best yielded to, as if by right.
Bikes tick up the small roads,
we greet those who return
from the great fort, amused by the glitter
in their eyes, a strident satisfaction.

But up there, something happens.
For some, vertigo,
the sense of fall and rise at once,
sucked and held as no birth-tunnel
ever did. We are at the front line. Here
things dance and tilt with light and dark,
with halo and hoof, with what is sealed
and what is cloven.

Later, at rest on a white beach,
sand threads through our pale toes,
black sea-water grips like death,
just beyond us. We imagine ourselves
as things we had not known; angels, devils,
the succubi of a sun-frozen shore.
In thrall to tides, winds, we contest
those moments of our lives.
Too late.
The banished gods proved wrong.

Turn, Season

Stocks are pared to the core.
Truth will out. The cupboard hoards small, silent
breads.
My stomach shrinks.
At dusk, signs flow in thin jets
of flailing branch, my lover
is leaving for an unknown country.

Each day is a countdown, every leaf
hurls towards winter on the wind,
like ticking clocks I do not want to hear.
The hour will come, so the leaves say,
the quarter-hour and minute,
even the second will come when the sky
falls through bare branches.

Then my shoulders will sink
beneath the weight of a dying part,
I will hide my face,
lie low like an animal.
Cupboard doors fly unhinged,
release the staleness of borrowed days.
In the market place,

women barter for the past's
clear forms. I pass by, find shapes
set aside in the bustling space,
hand over my coins
to buy what is priceless:
new breads for the stomach,
an astute lover for the soul,

a sabre tooth for the bite of death.

Caretaker

Of journeys, visits,
    a ring he gave me once,
        bottles, mystic signs

on the back of pictures
    that only she could decipher;
        of days and that unanticipated hour,

the sound of him on his way to her.
    His things, his smells,
        fresh every morning,

the light waft of night sweat,
    his arm flung across her,
        a sudden dream cry, night vision

of a marauding dog,
    the way his feet find hers,
        deft and searching as hands,

how their toes curl and fit,
    all of it packed tightly down
        to a clasp at break of day.

Tarsal

I came to the world with weights on my feet.
Childhood helped me bear the load.
I scarcely felt the leaden drag,
deftly fitted to heels, arches,
undersides of toes.
Sometimes, in dreams, wings sprouted
from my shoulders,
or behind my knees, small distractions.
In dreams, there was flight at ceiling level,
or down the stairs. Wings unclipped,
I gusted the length of local streets,
a liberal angel, greeted the cabbage-seller,
Fair Day farmers, a white-haired fortune-teller,
averted my head politely from the vagrant,
his threadbare coat slung wide,
who whispered, like a Beatles chant
gone wrong: I'll get ya! I'll get ya!

But the weights began to know me.
Cyclical dullness at first; later, insistence.
Like the nun's tuning-fork, at choir:
a raw thread, binding,
drawn the length of the body, pulled taut.
There were no pills for lead-bound feet,
for soldering irons, the silent clang
beneath, pulling, pulling.

I saw how the wind determined
the shape of a tree, took refuge in cosmetics,
the shape of my own full lips,
primed to kiss, laugh, soften.
Only when the cut crescents of toenails

rushed down the plug-hole,
when I was shaved, powdered, painted,
did I have what it took to survive in that town
where even the streets bent to stare,
and houses had cute, country eyes,
too hard to trust.

Palms out, I palpated the surface,
seeking soft belly, porousness, a welcoming kinship.
In time, I discerned the capacities of air,
what flowed up, or down, like invisible flutes
tuned to a medium of flight,
the resonating om in belly, heart, crown.

The ones I feared no longer touched me:
neither cabbage-seller nor vagrant –
his three whispered words died like a bad joke –
nor was I hostage to the crumpled fortunes
of a tea-leaf reader with nicotined hair.
I erected within a monument
to pain, the feet that bound me,
to the unwalked, unflown, unweathered.
I moved through, felt first feathers,
tarsals sprouting for flight.
An elision, knowing there were no walls,
just membranes. I unlearned gravity
phase by phase. I slipped through.

Solstice

Clouds have cleared. The Wicklow mountains
undecked of weeks of rain, leave
liquid ledges that overspilt the carping skies.
On this final day of the sun's trifling
with veils of moisture, low horizons,
there is light above – not the hopeful shaft
of a megalithic dawn, the silence in grave passages
as it steals through, then fades prematurely –
but a full six hours with earth and sky
revealed like chiaroscuro.

The lakes stretch out in loops,
like the eyes of slowly blinking water gods,
shorelines knotted with submerged boats,
as the ground squelches and soaks, but the sky
is a clear patch on the canvas of the global north,
mountains are semaphores, blue-grey signals
brushing open air, inviting light to enter and re-enter
streams, crotches of trees, the pores of our skin.
We are fully pleasured.

How the Tongue Reads an Apple

Now the apples are dreaming
of strange sugar, of bounty as never before.
The pale pink innards of Beauty of Bath
are saturated, already plump with syrup;
unearthly acids provide just the right tang,
held back, restrained as the sun-borne sugars
whittle deeper through the skin, and still nights
act as sealant. Dawn, a voile hammock,
holds the burst globes, the wet fruits,
until tongue tastes flesh, cunning-sweet
aroused, the darts of bitterness, caress.

Summerhouse Dream

Our first house is rented.
Mauve bedroom walls, thin curtains,
windows open while we make love in the daytime.
We joke about the bachelor next door,
his heavy footsteps on uncarpeted stairs,
the girlfriends we wish for him.
The kitchen sink is always blocked on Sundays,
when families visit. I long to forget
gravy and grease, to stroll
through the cornfield across the road,
be part of its yellowness.

*

In house number two, we learn
how dreams are spiked by mortgages.
I remember the predatory smiles
of jogging women, committee women,
experts in killer sports:
every passing year the older ones
ease the balls off their men,
slip them from the sac of innocent lust,
just by talking, talking. Some days I sweat,
frightened by the violent suburban silence
behind all the words.
Our walls offer no respite.

*

Later, I dreamed of a summerhouse, with octagonal walls,
a view of the sea. I tried to lay foundations.
It would be a place for making good

the snags, for rendering till smooth, for bedding down
before uncurtained windows.
Two shells curled together
on a gull's wing grey blanket.
Not even the ocean would part us.

My Irish Picasso

A single early work dumped in a closet,
a matador, the maddened bull,
those split shoulders and spurts of blood
as unseen crowds go wild.
Tenderness wanders the matador's arched back,
attends to the male strut imposing its will.
Lust is everywhere. In the ruby cape,
the streaming blood, the hot dust he forgot to paint
around demonic hooves, just where they bite
into the earth, then twist with pain,
bringing the vast head down, the fleshy snout
with its crown of trailing blood.

There is never enough time, my Irish Picasso says.
Forty years ago, his eyes were elsewhere,
searching for colour, texture, yet missing
the telling detail. Around him fragments,
assemblages: a cube of a woman's head,
oblongs of children, angling each effect
on the canvas. Here too is his daily bread,
the half-drunk coffee, dregs and sediments.
His bed, the sheets taut, so neat
he would never have imagined
what was tucked around a marriage,
the parts not amounting to a whole.

Now Guernica surrounds him.
The deaths, local, but inevitable.
A woman's head mangled by the violence
of what he never painted. He drives the children,
their oblong lives, away from the canvas.
Dust obsesses him, ochre, tawny, cinnamon,

that first and unrisked element.
In a frenzy of renewal, he seeks his Mediterranean,
the stuff of middle earth, myth.
Volcanoes on his palette,
fire gods and lava, he remembers hooves,
the bull's final agonies.

Tropical

1.

In this place, they do things differently. She
is no longer transparent, mad, or both.
Her children still live in the Tropic
of Cancer, their elongating bones lean
into her dreams, the Northern cool of continent
bodies. It almost draws her back, back,
remembering the bridge on her daughter's nose,
the blue logic in her eyes puzzling
incipient womanhood, amazed at her mother,
who presents a riddle neither can solve.

She tells herself the heat is nothing special:
her tropical body is all equator now,
right for her time of life. All those years
of being an Alpine spring, streaming on frozen
villages, gone! Now she takes back time,
not blood, though there is less of both.
In tropical repose, travels south
through seven time zones. Daily, enjoys
the sun-sleeked men, like watchful chameleons
on every branch, changing shy skins to suit her mood.

2.

Indistinguishable, because she was one
of them, women of comedic, scripted meals, women
of moving mouths, she hears the prescribed mantras,
Prozac, Prozac, Prozac, and HRT; she
listens to what is offered, and what withheld.
It shocks her still: those drives to supermarkets
after work, trolley-pushing, then the set
faces of other drives, her own set face

caught in the mirror. Lights dimming into dusk,
she moved reliably out and up the road to home.

Now there is distance. In this new heat, she sits
surrounded by greenery, tamarind seeds
hanging near her head. She cuts a mango, bites
and sucks, a glutton for all the sweetness of the tropics,
the earth turns inside out for such a taste…
This journey is an Open/Return. Remembering,
her feral eyes narrow, the place she left
a speck of darkness in the distance.
Overhead, the Pole Star drills ice into her brain,
as if to compensate for the milky
heat of equatorial nights. If she goes back,
her North will be a gaping mouth,
devouring the frail bones of what remains,
exposing the bits which never did comply.

The Library of Silences

Like any collector, you begin way back with choice pauses,
  sold to the covetous bidder. You ignore
  most of the Enlightenment, head for 20th century
  reel-to-reel absences, store the vintage gems:
  that priceless, Edwardian silence before sleep,
  or sepia silence after a question with no brakes,
  all Art Nouveau romance, like an infant
  automobile at rest in a new century garage,
  sure of the future before it turned monster.
  You catalogue the psychedelic silence between toads
  in a Sixties summer ditch, then back to Egyptian silence
  as you and he drift on a river through the tomb
  of a night-jungle – yours alone.

Some heavenly silences are shelved high up,
  barely within reach, deliberately symbolic;
  the silence between a sleeping child's breaths,
  which has no category in space-time, the edges of air
  feathery, dewy, bearing the shape
  of clean, elastic lungs; the silence during a Godard
  film, when the head swims with shape-shift
  colour, the silence beneath a crow's wing,
  reminding you of witches, warts, good women;
  the silence of when the bus stops, Newtonian silence
  as an apple drops towards the ground,
  the unevolved, limbic silence of lust;
  the silence after Christmas, when you wear
  January's restorative shawl.

Daily, your finders on the slender shelves, cataloguing,
  rearranging. You bless silence. It brings fortitude,
  trims your soul to the shape of a time beyond the self:

a million galaxies, turning, spilling gravitationally
to one end. Only then is the passage from being young
to older eased. Silence. That horizon. The future.

The Place of Miracles,

The Place of Miracles

When the big man fills my grandmother's doorway
in 1959, uncles move forward, arms outstretched.
In the background, a near-blind old statesman
whispers. Grandfather, *Papa*, has died. Women
stand by; teapots ready as Dillon the politician
steps inside the house of huddled dreams, where men
run the show and tongues are quick and cutting.

Four summers on, I swing on the hinge of De Valera's
dream, visiting Castlelyons, Cork.
I hear Munster voices, the circular warmth
of their joy at meeting an Ulster cousin
who prances in a blue, white-collared dress
chasing and chased before high tea, mounds
of ice-cream, sweet stewed apple, twirls of cream.
Shadows laze around the house.

I'm not as free as I thought, the weight of a sibling
not felt yet on my shoulders: *South Anne Street. Dublin,*
Catholic Protection and Rescue Society of Ireland:
My infant sister, her pink bud face in the adoption room,
six-month-old fingers tugging at her hat
as we rattle home from Dublin. Grandmother
and mother share her in the back. This, I am told,
is Margaret Veronica.

What I recall is the crying on her first morning,
the screaming, the struggle to bathe her in the big Belfast
kitchen sink, my mother wrestling a squirming soapy
infant, alone in her duties, head bent, no longer
seeing the laurel hedge outside, the high field
that shouldered gently over the house. I am witness

to her grace, the absence of some word of help. No angels
announcing for her, a husband at work, sisters
and brothers busy filling their own nests.

Weeks later, a social worker calls, examines,
smiling with my mother at infant progress.
The child is fine, that smile conveys, mother
is well and as the months begin to tease
there is strangeness in the air.

Spectres that will haunt forever: how we lived
parallel lives, believing families were a well-knit garment,
all of us like dropped stitches, undone among our ancestored
worlds, feeling ourselves central, generous
to the tail-ends of another gene-pool.

Sisters and yet not. Six years between us. I am too old,
she too young. We are no use to one another.
In my child's way I see the little one, pitted against
cousins in the house of huddled dreams. Grandmother's
house, where aunts, uncles, congregate and change
nappies, feed gobbling spud-shaped babies as the clan expands.

Two infant girls, one of them my new sister, struggle
for possession of a handbag, goaded on by adult
watchers. I sense something unpleasant, a whiff of
sides being taken, shitty and primordial, glee-filled
tut-tuts when the other child is stronger, claims the bag,
and my rage-scalded sister dissolves. Not one of us. Not yet.

We move on, paths still separate, come together for meals,
walks. Sometimes mother plays a red vinyl record,
Christopher Robin and *The Teddy Bears Picnic*.
Margaret Veronica dances, later

picks out tunes on a toy piano. In years to come
her *Pathetique* will fill the house, and mother —
as if in recompense for untold stories —
buys *Sheherazade* as a gift.

*

On my own journey, caught in the middle,
a river inspires a first song. *Oh Blackwater,*
Blackwater, hummed from the bridge near
the Co-op, after the walk past Simpson's gate
with father, smell of the buck goat, its impudent, alien-
shaped pupils staring from between bars.
The river breaks musical secrets, unworldly bells,
tucked beneath emerald weeds
slashed with yellow, hemmed to the stem
of marsh marigold, glistening on backs of fish.
I see a kingfisher, a lightning blue stream,
caught peripherally. I sense yet do not know
where that river runs, how it slides slowly to the moist
folds of an Ulster lough and another life, currents
separating in the province of the tribes. The river
brings peace: the Monaghan river, wet channel of my life.

When I go to boarding-school, sister sleepwalks.
They find her, trance-like, in the kitchen, playing
with a new kitten in the autumn dawn,
I, her mute bulwark, no longer present
when she emerges from her morning straggle
of blanket and tatty hair.

On a Wexford beach in '67 she wanders off.
My father, I can almost hear his panicked
heart as he runs the length of Fethard strand to find her,
feel the ache in his soul, the possibility that she

is lost to us. But all is well. She who wandered is found,
prodigious daughter in search of roots.

Suddenly I'm grown. Humanities-educated. Married.
Away from Monaghan. Nothing works
in the new sparse house. Windows keen
in the winter of Maynooth, *Nuada's* plain
demythologised as houses creep, moist
as mushrooms in the night. In the village,
roofs shoulder fog from the canal. I am displaced.

Locked in a new dream of Bergman and wolves, of
Bertolucci, Bunuel, warm dust and sex, I flee my kitchen
to the city, searching, searching. Behind me,
the mill whines and drones. Around me, ideas bob
like fallen blossom on the surface, floating, seedless:
gossip is of clingfilm for double-glazing and condoms,
home-made wine, camden tablets, the price of love vertiginous.

In five-o'clock dawns beyond our bedroom, the Asahi train
slowly shunts through as if by stealth, sneaking liquid toxins
to a Mayo factory. Other trains drum along, not daring to stop
in a village where Charlie Haughey's young dreamers
struggle in knots of hope.

*

But in Monaghan, word of death on its way: the flag
goes up, the flag comes down again. Bobby Sands
is fading fast and the black rectangle flutters over the Co-op.
Come every morning, it shivers stark against bone-white sky.
Milk delivered, silos filled, cheques issued. The manager,
my father, detached to the last, watches the flag go up,
come down, go up again. A balancing statement,
either way, in need of utterance. Beside the Co-op,

the Blackwater wends on to the Bann, shadowed
by lime trees, and the row of poplars he once planted
to bring life to the place.

Although I left, I never leave, still impaled
by what I know. *Mary Elizabeth* and *Margaret
Veronica*, sister and sister, we interrogate the past
and now the runes are clearer. Through the years,
jousts of 'I remember, I remember ...', endless, stormy,
unpredictable. Blame is in the air, stand-offs subtle
and less so, we gallop towards one another,
each bearing a lance that hurts or heals.
I remember what she has searched for but cannot
bring to mind, uncertain feeling trails her, spying
every move. Other finds delivered from my bunker:
a photograph of her at four in Dún Laoghaire, our holiday,
alone with mother. There we sit, aliens
in plaits and swimsuits, before a camera too obscura
to penetrate our poise.

She leaves and returns, then leaves again,
bohemian bag-girl of the seventies, eighties, nineties,
yo-yos to and fro on her own long search. When booze
claims her, I watch, listen to the domestic rant
as parents try to get her to recant.
Here she triumphs. Here she is Samaritan,
neither bleeds nor weeps, but turns wild roots
to the souls of others; gives counsel while burning
the candle at both ends, sticking both thumbs
in the flame for the relief of pain and giving.
What Veronica pauses — what muslin of words
wipes the generational stain, breaks a running code
of misrecognition? It takes a life to learn kith, kin,
to bend, amoebic,
beyond the primordial taunt of family.

And still I write from the place of miracles: that some
found a guiding spirit, looked up, saw the colour
of love in a father's eyes, that religion did not
define, that the life-force was not always
sent howling on its way.

Return to walk the Vale Road, long relieving walks
in the evenings before father's death. For distraction
I try to memorise Chaucer's Prologue before the bedside
watch begins. How calming those first eighteen lines
of springtime and hope, young sun, tender crops and
rising Aries, a world of *swete breeth*, melody-crazed fowl.
En route, I meet the children of people I once knew,
features sure as a little stream
passing in the effortless spill of genetics.
It's in a gait, the set of someone's back,
those loaded silts swelling the pores
as our father's life is fading.

The truth of Margaret Veronica rises still in a vision,
wielding a hatchet in childhood, teased
to attack the kitchen door, her cheeks flooded.
Other, shed ghosts: my own, whiter, mood
buried in the bunker of my being, rarely released to light
until later; a turbulent gypsy-mother,
calling to the harmonising note, teaching intensity;
a father holding court, charming with
the poetry of his life; my sister again, and I, teaching
ourselves the strokes of sisterhood before it is too late.

Up there, Ulster-bound, down here Leinster-wise,
we hold fast and live. Steady. Steadfast.
Making daily poems of the ordinary.
Moon and sea weave a spell of shadows, currents,

light falls where least expected. In the end,
we give it all up — life, love, hate, the lot,
our disintegration unstudied, material,
as cell by cell, we tumble into wetness, absorbed
and absolved. *That we may shed our sins,*
not carry their print, cellular, into the waiting dark, that
I may remember a poem and sing
of a forgiving river winding North
from Monaghan.

Tattoo

Sometimes I'm a girl in boots
With blue tattoos on her thighs,
Crossing the city,
Finding him in the long red car
Where I murmur quietly,
Leaning in the window,
The wind skinning my white arse,
Blowing the pleats of a short,
Short skirt in a fan
Around my hips.
   Though his lips
Try to shape themselves around
The script of my tattooed thighs,
Truth is, neither he nor I
Learnt to read hieroglyphs
When it would have been easy,
When what we saw was suppressed,
Those massed, ephemeral, butterfly-wings,
Alive with colour, determined
To stir the space between thighs.

The Bare Branch

When the branch is bare,
think of your limbs, think
of your spare skin,
its unclothed odour.
Light longs to lay itself
against you, there, there,
where you stand at the mirror;
light wants to caress your notched trunk,
those nipples, that navel,
the constellations of moles,
to move over the welts of bra-straps
to the soft bark of your shoulders,
to curve around your waist,
over the imprint of floor-flung pants.

When the branch is bare,
run your fingers down the slopes of your sides,
into the cleft of your buttocks,
or into the clip of the groin,
then south to the plump mound
where the thigh blossoms.
Invade your nostrils, your ears,
pursue the trail of every orifice north
and south. See yourself, fleeceless,
unpreened, entirely criss-crossed
with internal pathways, a miracle cosmos
where the cells are planets that spin on,
and on, regardless.

Return to Clay

It is not hard.
Go west or south, north,
east if you wish. Take
the swift path to the soil,
in boots or killer heels,
dungarees or velvet. The garments
are irrelevant, merely
a beautiful counterpoint
to the moment when you sniff
the air, realise your pores
have filled with the smell of clay.
Let clay drive out all dangers
that prey on you at night.
If needs be, kneel down, speak
to the earth about your burden,
ask it to share the great weight
you cannot bear in solitude.
The earth will accept you.
It will not judge your frailty,
nor torment your weakness.
There is no shame in being tired,
or anguished, in feeling fear
when your ears are bursting
with the wrong sounds.
Let the earth hold you: be a child
again. If your mother never held
you, if your father could not touch you
without shrinking, speak to the earth.
Lean in close, feel the strong arms
of old clay – powdered, heavy,
wet, wormed – feel
what knew your nature
before you knew yourself.

Ritual of the Blackberry

As the juice trickles along my fingers, I smell
flavours, tangs. Each berry comes replete
with its own idea of co-existence. Some
hang heavy as a noble grape, roll lazily,
willingly into the palm of the hand; others
resist at first, then fall loose, releasing acid
in the mouth. Decisions of taste: no blackberry
is an island. Each stem curves up and out
into a hoop, seeking ground again, the religion
of roots. The network continues along the road,
year after year, despite muck and cars,
frost and drought. In the end, what matters
is the harvesting, the savouring. My basket heavy,
they drop in plumply from the wickered hedge.
Blackberry of dark sugar, blackberry
of incensed dusk, blackberry so round it is
a black globe of a hundred gleaming globes,
seeking difference, distance.

Meditation

1.
Autumn, her season.
Two have left, like children
in a sap-translucent past.
She has a passion for her own time,
transfixed by sienna leaves rushing
into the horizon,
sunsets like incinerated cities,
places where she once worked
and hurried, lunched
in the Green with friends.

Her own time needs her.
While the waters in her head see-saw
with songs, one question tags her:
How to approach. To knock
or write – a crucial note
perhaps – promising pills or ropes,
if only death will have her.

Death means winter. Already
the final season, prospecting.
It will bend over her,
all kindness and ice.
Beyond her imaginings: lying down
in white, skin flecked with the milky crystals,
like feathers, the hot, angry blood
absorbed by snow-drifts.

2.
What holds her to autumn
are these clusters of children.

Her daughter – visiting friends –
their darting eyes as they rake the muck
on teachers and boys. Already,
acorn breasts are rising,
nails are long, armpits
rank with sweat.
They need her to impart
some wild template from the past,
though what she knows
is mystery.
A few phrases on following the dream,
something half-understood
about liking themselves.

It helps to invoke the girl-wraiths
of her past, distant seasons
when she was luminous,
when her eyes or hands were gentle,
or her laughter. She conjures up
her first, gagging kiss,
the vile slug of a stranger's tongue
in her mouth, and tells her daughter

the difference between that kiss
and a later, sweeter flame,
the heart-crushing beauty of the world,
the dews, lights, the shifting wetness.

The Swimming Pool

Breathing out before the plunge,
we sink deeper each time, free-falling
to the bottom. Down there, we mimic
the contours of imagined lives:
yogis, lotus-limbed in prayer –
heaving water tilts us askew,
like statues toppled from
cliff to ocean. We find speech-
nodes in finger signs, make frantic,
bubble-punctuated jokes until
lungs are burning, ears roar,
we torpedo to the surface.

Expelling air, we sink again,
no longer daughter or mother.
Playmates instead, sharing prodigious
lore of the unmarked regions.
Indifferent to a coming kingdom,
she fin-flicks an empyrean
realm of pregnant sea-horses,
at ease with the neptunian slobber
of spore and dreaming filament.
Eight feet down, age has no ballast,
the pressure on lungs and heart
gives room for deliverance.

Both of us, flicking feet like tails,
balance for future and past
as we pull at one another.
Hauling equal weight, freed of
the usual gravities, we inspect
our mutual kingdoms:

one well-trodden, another, still
replete, pink as a mermaid's coral comb.
It opens as if to a set pace,
aware of a shore searching her out,
offering the earth if she will have it.

The Great Stink

Shameful things, as ever from the east: typhus, cholera,
And now air you could cut with a knife, the Thames backed up
To the Lambeth ditches. Politicians, urged at last
By heat, flies, fleas and ticks, breeding dysenteric legions,
Scribble behind scented sacking in the House of Commons.
I, Bazelgette, free at last to implement the plan
I trust but have not proved. Citizens die beneath yellow
Miasma, solids spreading, deepening, the floating bulk

Seeping into mud, shingle, the great water itself.
My calculations being correct, this will be the miracle
Of our age: freedom from ordure, directed into continent
Channels, egg-shaped as befits what is unbreakable,
Entering the river east of the city, ferrying
All end-work to the ocean. I see the men – ready
For eighty-three miles of Portland brick – the toughest –
Coughing, hacking their way to build the interception that

Will solve it. All summer, ladies in humid houses insist
On roses, roses, in doorways, vases, upon their breasts;
Cologne for the gents. Fatigue abounds. But nothing conceals
The odour from the poor, who endure and die. My task
Remains to organise effluvium, send it on its pungent way,
Concreted, mortared, in a serpentine dream of dissolution
Despite the wettest summer of the century, the river
Rolling beneath jeering vapours. God bless the fragile

Web of planning and construction as we check
And re-check the scale of containment and discharge. New
Embankments in my sights – Victoria to the north,
Albert to the south – to further block the leakages.
Come winter, the men's hands harden. Earth is frozen

As they dig and dig again until tunnels meet
Precisely beneath the pumping houses, belly
Of the network, Abbey Mills, Deptford, Crossness, working

Monuments to the passage of my faith. As ever,
The people fish the river – drink, breed, sleep and shit –
Undeviating as the sewers now driving the stuff
Beneath marsh birds, gulls, bearing stink, pestilence,
Ancestral shame along secret currents of extinction,
Creating distance between mouth and arse, packing
The intestinal load within the membrane
Of the city: Dark. Utilitarian. Starless.

Note: Joseph Bazalgette was one of the most distinguished civil engineers of the Victorian era. He built eighty-three miles of 'interceptory' sewers that prevented raw sewage from running into the Thames, believing (mistakenly) that the foul-smelling 'miasma' that hung over the river was responsible for death by disease and not the untreated solids in the same source that was used for drinking water.

Birches in October

Layers of air pass over,
rings of ancestors pressed within.
Branches curve. Grey, sparing,
nautical. Life is struggle, they say,
but there are consolations: seek
what covers you, the canvas
that sheaths the hull,
your own colours and textures.

The trees would blaze again if they
were painted. How they would speak
to the men, the women, who carry
the load of so many seasons,
who wait for a clean fall of snow.
Pliant, branches that dipped down
in summer now rise above themselves,
intent on voyage. Leaves faithful
to the cooling sky, drop invisibly
during the night, nudging out
to the curling, noiseless tips. Fallen.
Another season driven out to sea,
leaving land, making room.
Time folding over.

Speed

I want you to walk faster.
To forget that you cannot keep up, that
the time for keeping up is sharpening
to an end. A point often lost on me.
Arrows abound. Branches lash
the night outside your room, anchored
miraculously by the weight of that
winter-whittled trunk;
eighty miles away I worry about
power cuts, whether there's a box
of matches beside a candle near the bed.
You speak of midnight relief, a glass of milk,
your sleeping-pill, being perched
against pillows, television on, then
the ritual of night prayer from a book he used
in his last months. He sometimes visits, you say,
have woken in the night, or at dawn, sensing
someone at your back. It is all slow, so slow,
no hurry at all. Outside your window
the garden creaks and clicks into the day.

Wilderness Legacy

I leave two books, as promised.
The Buddhist one on suffering, and
The Rubayyat of Omar Khayyam,
for the sake of a verse about
a loaf of bread, a jug of wine
and *'thou beside me in the wilderness'.*

For myself a dream of the Isle of Isla,
imagined from long ago, cottage
near the sea, black dog to guard me
when I wasn't communing with Gallic poets.
You, occasional visitor to my wilderness,
would bring an extra seam of light,
that indefinable male gleam, itself a speech-
form conversing with my body.

Mostly it's wilderness I seek. Buddha
can't ungrow the harvest of suffering.
When you read the *Rubayyat* you'll know
the huge joke on all of us, will sense
a ruthless finger, its protracted prodding.

To the shore now. The black dog
waits. He loves the way I smell
and how I speak to him.

The Derries, 1976

Photos show me in shorts, acting the farmer, pitching
a twist of hay onto raddled cart, hair haloed, light itching
my skin. It wasn't the place for a tryst, your father's land
a mile beyond the tunnel bridge, those few days, hand-

braided by ourselves, with tricks and contrasts, a dark hayshed,
smell of straw in the flecked bower when the old man was led
far away, a speck on the bog's brown tide. The freest time:
my body tingled with all that lay ahead, a blind sublime

eye reading to the future. Even rapture deceives, never
as imagined, the world still spinning; I see you lover, as ever,
worrying about being caught in thick clouds of hay, our haunt,
I, laughing my head off at the notion, foreseeing the jaunts

I'd lead you on, the naked swims, unchoreographed, wine-
drenched dances, my best, my precious gift, a refusal to toe the line.

Exiles

1.
Girl from the East, Palmerstown traffic-lights.

She swings between steaming morning cars,
one trouser leg doubled back above the knee,
her main business, *The Big Issue*, clamped
beneath her elbow. A squall of snow
bears down just when the eye is drawn
to the omission: a metal pin, her stiff bird gait,
a crutch. A cloak of ice billows over windscreens,
bullets of hail lodge in folds of her blown-back
hood. Her forehead is knotted against such force
that shreds air   sky   time
        A single footprint, clone of the one
before, visible on the ground, and black discs in snow
from her crutch, like inverted commas before
and after every footprint, track the script
of her labour.
        Drivers in snoozing cars register the matter,
faces inscrutable, stall briefly at the gleaming pin,
the raw air below her thigh. Somewhere
in Romanian earth,
        the molecules of her incinerated limb have
        reformed.
        Here, she is at war with deficit.

2.
Alex in the Garden

In his homeland, a builder. In Ireland,
he sweeps the piled sheddings in my mother's garden,
the sinewy fen of his body spreading to reach
lacey drifts from lime, sycamore, larch.

When he weeds, he scoops beneath the roots,
leaving no evidence of a plant's history; when
he paints a trellis, it is saintly, Vilnius white.
On Sunday evenings, icons appear in the open
rhombus spaces between crossed slats of wood:
St Stephen, other martyrs. In the field above
the house, a stoat flashes, white as snow.

He leaves *Koruna* chocolate, photographs of his wife
and daughters flaying birch-branches after *sauna*,
himself on cross-country skis. His whiteness struggles
for survival in the red speech of our North, he
tries to match his landscape to the stranger's, pondering
aloud, 'What is this number, this number *ee-yit?*'

He has shaped shrubs like Eastern spires nestling
in snow, thick-shouldered and undauntable. But
when my father died, he shed fat tears
at the wake, they flowed unashamed,
watering his roots and ours.

3.
The Final Shrug

The Russians have come, the world has not stopped.
Ivory-cheeked, blond, their blue eyes blaze
with things we never knew. They shop decisively
for cut-price familiars: beetroot and celeriac,

horseradish, tinned pork, violent mustard.
Their fertility makes a boisterous fire.
The Russians have come, rangy as wolves,
their mouths and wide eyes, their busy movement

stoking a pain we may not wish to feel.
Neither pilgrims, nor helpless, their shopping
is a choreographed dance away from one-roomed
apartments, from dachas, hunts by night, peasants and hound

working as equals. We wait in the check-out queue,
trolleys creaking with packs of German biscuits, rye
bread, Polish beer. Regard our unsacred lurch away
from history, as we wait, and wait. See the

dark font of legendary slops, our efficient handling
of what we have learned together. The Russians have come.
They are with us as we shrug it all away, the old pain
of never having, the empty cupboard, the unfed hounds

of our countries howling at the moon for something, anything

4.
Old Roman Towns

The roof tiles on the new extension
are the colour of crushed peaches

grown in the foothills of a volcano.
Inside, men twist pipes, steel girders

support the ceiling. What drew us
to break walls, adding height and light?

This is a necessary space,
the new romance of brick and stone

we hankered for twenty years ago,
in Yugoslavia. We looked down

from the hills on old Roman towns,
drank in the mineralised heat

that radiated from the roof-tiles.
This was how to live, we thought: passionate

beneath a roof the colour of rich earth,
overlooking cobbles where people

met at evening near the sound
of an antique fountain.

Now we know differently.
It was not, after all, how to live,

as tribes of the Balkans drowned
in blood. So, in the speckled wars,

slouching beasts tearing the earth,
what drew us to rebuild? We extend

ourselves closer to birch and ash,
hearts more urgent than ever as the wind

rolls in from the west. What jeopardy
inside these walls and windows,

whiskey on the table,
bare feet stretched to the night fire?

5.
Poetry Reading, Irish-Polish Society, Fitzwilliam Place
evening of the 60th Anniversary of the Liberation of Auschwitz

The signs are auspicious: twisted brass supports
a chandelier, a hanging, ochred basin.
Bulbs glow within. On the walls, a crimson phoenix,
a huddled Polish farmhouse in black and white.
To my left, an iconic Mother of Christ, in blue,
gold and red. The fireplace tiles are blood-hued.
Whisperers gather, as if in church.

We smile our greetings, a city's oddities caring little
for race and pace, the fashion and passion
of the street, pinned together, genteel and awkward:
men with antique ponytails, women in baroque skirts,
safe in this chamber where all is liberation.
When the poets unleash the wolf of the imagination,
our ghost selves float above polder and plain,

over successions of invaders, where things happened
in secret. While the Irish railway shunted trippers
between towns and cities, Poland's *chemin de fer*
led standing millions to the chambers, unseen.
Yellow eyes, perhaps, witnessed death on the long poles
of smoke, would sometimes have drawn closer
to the rank odour of flesh not raw.

With us now, they wake in our minds again,
guardians of the unpaceable horizon, seekers
of crooked paths, far from the solution-makers.
In dreams, nothing is final and blood does not spill
behind averted backs: it washes, tidal, through the days,
warming and cooling to love's barometric fevers
as men fill wombs and children are born,

despite risen spectres, the unquiet ache
of a cut people. Later, there is tea, coffee, praise
for the poets, praise for fidelity. Knowing what can
go wrong, we choose oddness. Out of tune and time,
we file into the ashen night, opt for the long, drawn, note,
the howl in the wilderness. Hair-shirted in the cold,
we find a gift of bees, honey, the dripping, golden, combs.

The Confession of Agimet of Geneva, Châtel, October 20th, 1348, recounted by a Witness

Lent being over, he was dispatched after Easter
to Venice for silks and other wares. The snow
had melted. Content to make the journey, he rested
In the spring nights, safe beyond the towns and hamlets
of the Black Death. Now screaming, he faltered through
the vile story of a secret encounter with
Rabbi Peyret of Chambery, chief conspirator
among poisoners of Christendom, teacher of their law.
Willingly he took a package half a span in size, wherein
lay venom from the snakes of Africa, the edges
sealed with a woman's angelic stitching, he said,
all in a leather bag. *For the wells,* the Rabbi whispered,
for every Christian cistern and spring in Venice,
that the plague will claim the butchers, tanners
and nobles who borrow freely, then resent our gold.
Pour carefully, then cleanse your fingers
lest the particles are carried to your lips.
Let the Christians sip their last!

For this, rewards beyond his dreams. Thus Agimet
lightly bore poison to Venice; eyes glittering,
he scattered it into wells and fresh, sweet water.
Of his own diligence he left at once – spurred
by a Rabbi's promise! – for Calabria, Apulia, and poisoned
many cisterns. Nor did he demur before the fountain
of Toulouse where Christians clamour in the late sun,
and women and children fill ewers, and all the wells
near the Mediterranean Sea. This, the profligate poisoner
declared true enough for him to lay his soul on the five
books of Moses if proof were needed. All this
I heard and more, after torture, a little,
eased the truth from his breast.

The Cremation of Strasbourg Jewry, St Valentine's Day 1349

Our council knew no evil of the Jews of Strasbourg,
Though death went from one end of the earth to the other,
On that side and this side of the sea, and few
Were spared. Ships drifted on the tide, laden with wares
From distant parts, the crew dead, no one to steer.
Bishops, priests and monks, the good people of every kingdom
And city fell beneath the swift cut of the scythe,
Their skin burning black with disease. The pope at Avignon
Locked himself in terror in a room. Wise and foolish
Met the same end and the cause of the misfortune
Was clear to some, knowing how the Christ-killers,
The Jews, were reviled and accused in every land
Of procuring poisons and hoarding arcane knowledge.

But our council knew no evil of the Jews. In the end
Our bishop, the lords and other representatives
Rose against us, seditious mobs arrested Jews in thousands
On Friday, the 13th. Under torture most spoke out
And in towns along the Rhine the story of confessions
Travelled quickly. On St Valentine's Day, the wooden
Platform readied, the Strasbourg mob rounded up
Two thousand, sparing only those who wanted
To baptise themselves. The flames roared
High, driven by wind from the frozen mountains,
The screaming was unbearable. As an act of mercy
Many children were plucked from the fire and baptised.

All new Christians had to surrender pledges
Taken for debts, and cash and many precious things.
If they had been poor they would not have been burnt.
So great the burning that in some cities of the Rhine
The Jews themselves set fire to their homes, wailing

As they cremated themselves. *But our council knew*
No evil of the Jews of Strasbourg. It was decided
That no Jew should enter the city for a hundred years,
That Christians should sleep safe in the black forest of
Our ignorance and fear, but after twenty years,
In 1368 after the birth of our Lord,
The magistrates agreed to admit the wanderers again.
Our council knew no evil of the Jews of Strasbourg.

Lantern Light
for Wang Zhe Cheng

I pause as usual on the landing, forget the task in hand.
The moon is full behind the fretwork of a poplar.
In the pewter of a January night, I am flung back
to the surfer's paradise we briefly knew. You,
with your Chinese attentiveness, making a special expedition
to view the lunar reflection on the sea at Byron Bay.
'How's your man?' the apartment owner once jerked his head,

when I enquired about a writer's desk, smirking as Chinaman
and Irishwoman drifted in domestically, with groceries and books.
Together through the somnolent streets, we padded
beneath roosting parakeets, now silent in the tamarinds,
our words hesitant. Alone in the resort, stilted with native
cultures, we clambered then fell over mutual words, like rocks,
unsure of what would hold and what give way.

We circled one another. You thought me restless,
always walking, walking, Mary! I found your stillness
a stone to push against. You read me well, alert to the trouble
far away that kept me pacing street and beach That night
we did a Chinese thing: observed the lantern on the ocean,
sat and communed before flung fans of broken light. Pacific
waves roared to shore. Sand was damp, seagulls gone,

snakes tight beneath the rocks. Now at home,
I recall my life's moon-yearnings: the time the moon pursued
my parents' Morris Minor, or when I dreamed into its face,
reflected icily in Convent Lake, then later observed
the moulded hollows through a telescope. Tonight it shines
into the crevices of Ireland. Hours ago, it caressed
The Great Wall's stones and steps, the alleys of Shanghai,

the lotuses of Hong Zhou, where you – most likely – sit and
write. We never betrayed our sky companion, despite
the misused words, exiles, dividing walls, watch-towers
and book-burnings, distressed slogans of our tongues.
Through the trees, the past hovers, profusional.
Look, friend, at the little waves, our particled souls
afloat, waving at the shorebound yet to find speech.

Speaking in Tongues

1.
The Virgin Mary Shell
Inchydoney Strand

guests are warned to replace it should they find one.
a receptionist shrugs off the mystery,
remarking that it's rare

outside, a beach of latte sand gouache
    flickering gulls
because I do not search, I find
weightless in my palm, trove, voluptuous square
with rounded corners, now held to the sky, an offering
like the hip socket of an extinct sea creature

markings are miniature, ciphers, posted
from the Atlantic, a graceful 'M' pierced
on bone-white: rotate the shell to see
the vital 'V'

this is no Marian alphabet, but a vulva,
scored by an idle mer-boy imagining
the world of bifurcated beings oceanic
Síle na Gig, umber cunt beneath an 'M'

further along scallops clams whelks cockles:
discarded jewellery, flung aside in the toss where
waters meet, where getting to   retreating from land
nosing in   boning deeper   withdrawing again
before the tumult of a landing – is what matters
two tides, two pulses,
    iconic   erotic
        what we have
            all we need

2.
Have I Praised Enough

the things that made me
shapes of light roaming beaches, cloud-cloaks,

sudden honey harpoons over rocks,
because light owns space and is free to move,

on mountains,
reclining on roofs,

in sun and shadow play around your face,
or finger-work through your hair

or the sight of a tin can in a ditch, that mythic rust,
and amber reeds as dawn blooms

around low lakes
great water and great breath

making harmonies of humming
did I cry feeling aloud, make sufficient hymn

of the adventure? Trees, skies and patterns,
cosmic maps, fields folded,

tucked in by dripping hedges,
the body's workings, the human,

unmechanical odour, like incense to cross-hatch,
pollinate the avenues of play,

where lines do not narrow,
and there is no blind spot

what I saw, felt or tasted, over and over,
taken naturally that I could only speak

in poems as if in tongues
did I speak enough of such things?

3.
Naturists

If it was a matter of casting off clothes, it would be simple. Instead we choose silence. If we speak about a bright weed or spilt cerulean drowning the sky, it's on a need-to-know basis. Otherwise, we consent to splitting words with stranger and friend alike, hoarding what we know. Left to our own resources, we pass the time watching nuthatches, thrushes, analysing the etymology of utterance; we embrace trunks of trees, clothed or sky-clad, press our lips against furrowed bark, smell our way into the syntax of a thousand insects beneath the surface; sometimes, we spread our limbs on dolmens in the sun. We do that too when it rains, watching colour deepen when the stone is sodden, the hairs on our arms rising to greet the whisper of droplets, feeling water dribble along our shoulders, between the cleft of the breast, down to the lake of the bellybutton, slipping to the thatch of the groin, deep to the pink souterrain. Rarely do we admit to being electrified by nature, where the eye can rest, the ear sigh into sound, skin fizz to a passion that is human and fleshly in this elemental. Invisible things, to unburden the mind: the rhythms of seasons, January's awkward jig, the froideur of April bowing to May, when the pagan in us remembers ancient summers. Starting afresh, we hoist the maypole and dance. Suddenly it's June, August then the wild nights of Samhain. As naturists, we play it down of necessity. Who wants to hear us out, who'll talk to us on the loose, not be uneasy, as we spit white-hot flames? Too excited for our own good.

Taking the Mask

I.

I used to think it too easy. Describing it as a visitation by a wolf. Now, I'm not so sure. If I have rejected the creature for too long, if I have imagined it has fled back to the cold that suits it best, I am wrong. It arrives with bared fangs, whiskers quivering as the muzzle snarls. Its hackles are high, even before I enter the kitchen. The cast-iron stove clangs and breathes hotly, warming the winter room. A radio is tugging knots of sisal through my ears. I take my pills, dutiful to the hard pressure in my foot-bones, wrist-joints, knowing I am caught out, again. Already my head pounds in rage, the very thing countering the path of health. I have followed rules, taken meds, didn't even have to learn to be a private visionary. I have always found the links and paths I needed. Now I have to prove something more: how to close the gap to this companion, how to reach out as if to say *there, there*, how to stroke the creature into submission. It is the only way I know.

II.

I didn't have to learn to love the creature in the archipelago of my blood. *Love?* Accept, more like. I took the mask, thought I did so willingly, blew with gust and bluster, finding *lupus, lupus,* always waiting, attentive. This wolf always requires more. And more. Rest comes only when he has been filled, when he has led me North beyond trees and screes. Does the creature love, I wonder? Me and others of my ilk? His arrival, always silent. Somehow, in the midst of domestic comings and goings, somehow on all my car journeys to the city, somehow in the throng of book launches, readings, the occasional joyous meal at Sheila's salon on St Stephen's Green, somehow he finds me. With such silence, such stealth! He slouches on silk and thistledown, his path through is soundless. It's easy to ignore his maw's first fastening, tensile on ankles, wrists. Even the sting when I grip the steering-wheel and drive, the blood beneath forced to dance against nature, too viscous for the choreographed threads and alleyways of my fingers. I pretend the rhythms run freely, avert my gaze and look to the day's horizons, searching for massed ships beyond the shore. I'd like to meet them, awaiting bounty and reloading.

III.

For a time, snow-caps recede. A deception, of course. Now the creature's truly at my heels. Night falls. I wake to one wrist in the grip of jaws, the joint pierced, fingers paralysed. If I resist, the bite sinks deeper. If I pretend it's just a nip, he threatens to rip and worry. Ghost in my home, nothing for it but to sit below, sipping herbal tea after slurping back the steroids, to wait it out in the bay window, vaguely watching nets of stars above the house. Wrongly mapped, they have no bearing. I am slow as a specimen in formaldehyde, see no trajectory of escape. Thoughts of formaldehyde remind me of the pitch-pine workbenches of the science laboratory at school, and the experiment that went wrong when the science nun had instructed us to slow up the movement of a frantic little paramoecium, by using formaldehyde. We used too much. On the projected screen we observed our one-celled specimen, now frozen in a sea of red, the movement of microscopic cilia disabled forever while the nun frowned.

IV.

The wolf's within the corridors. When I say 'the corridors' of course I mean 'my' corridors. Howling and seeking, patient with hunger while I tinker with distractions: World Service news: tectonic disasters and yet more death. Sport and steroids. An article on the Taoiseach's former mistress. Her new life. Her dynamism. At that moment I almost laugh, then weep at the ardour of reportage rousing cosy people skin to skin in bed. Pain persists and will for days. The wolf prohibits cosiness. It's time, I know, to yet again attend. *Be free of guilt,* the long incisor twists, *beyond you, in you, every cell is coded.*

V.

Shut-eyed now, window-glass against my head, I rise above house, roof, trees. The wolf's possessed me, I belong to neither place nor nation, life converging to a speck on a frozen archipelago far from any ship: the bounty here is truth in stillness. The wind does not moan, air breathes on flesh, snow falls plumply as broken bread. Now part of this naked tracking, the wolf has his way. It is not a choice to smell hide – rank – feel textures, the rough and smooth, to hear the heart – steady – a guide and tempo-keeper, holding me to faith. In the light of snow, head graced in the minutes after darkness, uncrazed insomniac, I wait it out till my blood cools. The mandible relaxes. I wait, uncertain. When I inspect my face in blue pools of icy water, the mask is there, along cheekbones, across my pale nose, like white gold, the corners of my eyes daubed and tilted from the marks of ritual. Inside, I burn before the gods of animism, I speak in many tongues. Ageless, devoid of all the ornaments I crave and save, alone and sane in a wilderness of light. The boundaries dissolve, moon and sun hold steady in a sky of Limburg blue.

Eight Ways of Looking at a Crow

I

An old man, ragged as an uncle
on his way to Benediction, suddenly dull
at the end of his season, virginal,
the lone one at a distance from
the screaming flock above cut wheat.

II

A secret that wants to be outed,
wearing black like a new widow,
uneasy with the arrangement
of the sky after a spring storm. Hailstones
were not expected, nor ice from the north
chaffing feathers.

III

A signature of air, a tumbling
question-mark as the wind drops,
or an exclamation mark plummeting,
sharp as a black diamond into the soul.

IV

These inheritors are not meek.
The earth is theirs though they are
distant as God, aware of glinting
metal insects trailing long roads:
killer-machines.

V

Instant death is preferable
to a broken wing, a snapped leg:
see the grown nestlings gather,

shrouded, round black eyes aglitter
with the prospect of loss.

VI
The man would be wise as Solomon,
speaking without a magic ring, to
the crow. Perennial retainer,
autumn projectile shooting
below the clouds. Heavy as stones,
they fall, call, wild with socialising
when corn is cut and mice
are on the run.

VII
The woman is oracular, speaks
in runes near the edge of the garden.
In the mist, she hopes her white kimono
will dupe them, calm them. Motionless,
she waits for their inspection,
hears them call to one another,
like corner-boys or women standing
in sunlight, the world suddenly warm
as massed feathers.

VIII
Fly with us! Fly with us!
They do not really mean it,
but intention counts. A chance
to stand on hill, dolmen, cliff,
head tilted back, dipping up
to the lake of the sky, arms spread,
testing the wind, wondering.
Fly with us! Fly with us!

The Ghost of Me

Bless my soul but I am free.
This morning I know it,
burdens gone, gone, nothing
more on my mind than smoking
a couple of Nat Shermans.
I hear the trees speak eternal
things, flapping little fadings,
the pennies of death dropping
to the grass where, overnight,
spiders have woven shrouds.
Woo-ooooh!

Before

the time when cars have left
drives and garages
the world is an opened shell,
one half blue, netted with quiet cloud,
the other half green, leaves drooping
with dew, with wisteria, and whitethorn
clotting hedges all the way to the road.
Nascent, still attached to night's
umbillicus, my elementary eyes widen.

Your Heart

for Anna

A mansion where I stroll freely.
At the slightest touch, every door
pushes open, hinges clean, oiled.
Light floods the rooms where furnishings

are simple: chairs in truthful shapes
aligned to what is human, a broad wooden
table, its yellow grain waxed, set
for as many callers as can visit.

No formality here. We do not break
bread, feasting instead on strawberries,
meringues, drinks that fizz, in keeping
with your spirit. All is chasteness, joy,

antique talents. In the long hall,
cats and kittens whizz by, climb
sea-green curtains; your dog wheezes
and pants in a yellow splodge of sunshine.

Friends drift in and butterflies waver
through flung-back doors. There is
constant music, and one room
for silence. Your heart, a mansion.

The Flea

If I were one I could jump
over the Eiffel Tower,
somersault to the top of the
Grand Canyon. Easy then
for the flat black speck
to spring astronomical distances
from the mushroom pink springboard
of a rat's left ear, or the thicker pelt
between tail and anus, landing
on some rag of a garment
in which a boy is heading off to sea.

One Summer

Without imagination,
we could never have invented
this summer, our movements
like bright leaves nudged
by the wind's unstoppable breath.

Heat

Far north, the ice has given way. Those plunging
negative numbers are less certain of late though
entities dressed in white pelts still roam the kingdoms
of minus. Translation rights to unfrozen language
have been effected. A melt-down of symmetries
nears completion. Frozen blue, untranslated, means
safety, also horizon green, night purple:
fidelity to the mystery of speech, syntax.
Now the planet's heart fibrillates in the subtlety
of heat. Earth's hat and shoes have slipped loose, she is
vapoury with dementia. A huge gate
swings back, moisture flows, no longer set
or deep. North Atlantic Current, Gulf Stream, free to
cross-translate as ice wanders, melt-brained, incontinent,
across mosses, bogs, turning its back on the call
of terrible winter, what gave utterance to the
language of ice, its centuried stability.

Country Neighbours

High walls and hedges
make friends of them.
Heavy snow means parties,
shared candles in blackouts,
milk and bread broken
in the silence of
a winter evening.

Smooth roads and sunlight
make strangers. Two cars
mean independence. Sometimes,
we meet out walking,
but there is little to say.

Wise, Foolish Virgins

The Wise Virgins lost my respect
once they trimmed their wicks
ready for the Lord. Better
to have let the lamps blaze,
throwing gold-edged shadows
to the rafters as they kept good
company and wine flowed easily,
and Sabra stood in the fumey half-
light, her throat wide as she sang
a lament for love, her pet jackdaw
roosting above the thronged hearth.

Committee Man

An old dog, and the road is hard.
He has worn it smooth with time spent
nosing ahead, kept his tail wagging
meekly when the rest of the pack
were barking. He recognises
a cub on sight, the puffed-out chest,
the stiff gait, eyes trying to wear
nonchalance like a thick blanket
when all is transparent as nylon.
All he has to do is speak quietly
on the day, unforced, apparently
egoless. Advance preparations
serve him well, little mentions of
a name, dropped casually in the
middle of a conversation
about something else, directing,
altering the focus, gently,
a word here, a wink there, the right
memo at the right time. Those who
know him know he'll get his way.
Avuncular, benign, his brown eyes
glide towards the Chairman, concealed
by pouches of flesh. A done deal
before he opens his mouth.

The Last Weekend Before Secondary

It is the end of summer. Bats in flight
over the garden where four children wring
the day's final moments, shouldering nightfall
with a game of Tip the Can. As light retreats,
they have enlarged. One, still imagining childhood,
tries to be at one with three who are younger.
A separation has occurred, bafflement
bringing her to pause as she tries to catch
the shape of happiness. In two days, school gates
will open. She will enter with the other girls,
handling the balances of justice, beauty, kindness,
the barter of girls' worlds, sharp as swords.
But tonight, no abstractions. Just serene bats,
near-adult swallows tucking into mud nests
in the gable, four children screeching
beneath maple trees, savage and at ease.

New York Days

1.

It's Saturday evening and the boulevardiers
of Central Park South are rolling out in force,
buggy-pushing, the infant generation equipped
with vitamin-modified drinks and snacks
as their parents hold it all together beneath
fall-tinged trees, the sky above them still soft,
blue as a Limbourg painting. In that high cerulean
only a dragon is missing. Yet somehow,
iconic faces hang from the laced and glossy trees,
cut and decipherable in curling barks,
on outlawed branches about to be caught
short (any day now) by first frost.

2.

These buildings rush and dream, trailing bolts
of cloud from high plateaux. Blocks of light
are suspended like marble down the perspective
of Avenues, negative space is perfection
of the whole, air and colour nudge into every angle,
precise, as the high regal office plummets then widens
to street level, laying weight and dynamic deeper
into every storey, torso to hips and hips to feet
that grip the earth. A lesson in standing firm.
Someone, eighty years ago, took time
to ornament the block-work of a second floor,
some flapper-boy ensured that things
were more than simply lined and straight.

3.

In MoMA, we search the Jackson Pollock
for hidden screws and buttons, the sheer nerve

of teasing concealment – cigarettes, dimes
knotted in a texture of black, red, titanium,
a wormery of paint. He must have known
what held the world together was a matter
of small things: things that tighten, that close,
small change that makes the difference to our work,
here where youth's memorised equation,
the square of the hypotenuse being equal,
the mathematics of infinity
and the nature of an integer are
misconstrued aesthetics at odds with taught beauty.
Outside again, I light up and smoke, undo
a button, finger loose change in my pocket.

4.
Freed again from the predictable, this time it's
antennae all the way, no mad spiderish
scramble to understand it all. On Times Square,
I stand like any mesmerised country-woman,
then comes that old familiar rising of the self

from all that keeps me in my place,
against all that instructs on how to live
at fifty, as if the past half century
were infancy. I laugh at the remembered parade,
join now with feasting crowds out for the night,
spirits congregational, consensual,
my appetites already calmed though all
I've done is take a stroll and book a play.

5.
In the true South, they're talkin to the Fox
reporter bout God an his blessins, his
threefold blessins and how he'll save them from Rita,

daughter of Katrina. On the Weather Channel, we observe
her hurricane eye, the deep funnel bearing down
dispassionate, undecided where to fling
the contents of a vast and horizontal gullet,
how to further derelict what has been cut down,
releasing snakes and creatures of the underworld
from sewers, swollen rivers, as denizens of good and
evil march forth, paradise in jeopardy again,
and water, not for crossing over,
but for drowning in.

6.
It dawns on me this morning as I groan awake
to blades severing chinks in hotel curtains,
that Hamlet-like, I have thought, thought
but never done the one thing that I ought.
Outside, the city rises, yeasty dough
in a September fug. I do not want to go,
yet know I must, a day early, that I perceive
things to be held together as I pick my way
through what's to come, play for time
to gather all my small change, shift that sublime
hair's breadth forward, forward. All around,
conversational couples make warning sounds,
not unkind, not in judgement. The habit of holding
deep ingrained, all together, together as one,
yet pained. It will not do, of course, and I
am bereft. Brief consolation in a diner,
I gulp some coffee, then pick my way
through eggs and bacon, make small talk with the
waitress at her station, watch families and weekend
un-*chic* gals join together in this warmth.
Sex and the City it ain't, this glows unfashionable,
a pedestrian, golden breakfast on 6th Avenue,

weekend workmen, three or four, drill the sidewalk
outside the door. Later, I'll change my flight, book a cab,
edgy again, free to leave, to nab the morning's chance
when my heart's tectonics rip against each other,
the resulting electronics quietly unbearable. Even now,
I'm holding, holding, unable to let flow,
open my mouth so that you know, you,
dear friend who needs to hear my words. But I'll come
home. A half-century of living's not for dumbing-
down. I'll cross the ocean one more time, considering
the climate that I leave, the one that lies ahead,
where, for now, I must face down the congenital
root, land, suburb, parish, home. I've done my thinking,
mental gymnastics that cure nothing. If I were male
I'd maybe drop my '*home disputes*', then
hit the streets '*to cruise for prostitutes*', like Lowell
talking sense. But women just come home,
and now like some choleric Kathleen I'll cross the foam
and do the best I can with the compartments
of my life, what I'd gladly trade for tenements
if feeling – like chemistry – ran the route it should
and the pulse of love beat true, eternal and good.

Over Clongowes Castle

October crows in uproar,
six o'clock evening armies lay siege
to one another above slate and battlements.

The sky is a strategy of beak and wing
that spirals down to where I sit,
window open, in the car. Within,

boys are bellowing in the concourse,
so loud they almost drown these banner-flying
corbies in formation, army against army

in black hundreds, crossing through the sky
above the castle. Some reconnoitre
in the gaps between the battlements,

twitch wings, sharpen beaks,
prepare to fight again. Suddenly it's over.
They disperse as quickly as they rose,

back to a bunker of nests in lime-trees.
The dispute fades to *craw-craw*
conversation, desultory as twilight.

Dead leaves swirl and rattle towards gutters.
A door scrapes shut. Inside the castle, all is quiet,
boys, unknowing, at study for principles

of things to come: leadership, the cult
of uniform and strategy for men in black
or grey. The old priests settle

in a breathing-space between hours
– at desks, on chairs – lamps aglow,
the scent of decades on their prayer-books.

No uproar, yet still in siege,
the world gone eerily still,
beyond their hearing.